AF513311

Updated

Knowledge Lighthouse

A SKILL-BASED COURSE ON GENERAL KNOWLEDGE

6

Name : ....

Grade: .... Section : ....

Sustainable energy harnesses natural resources like wind, solar, and hydro to reduce environmental impact and ensure long-term energy security. Label these natural sources of energy.

Seema Chari • Kunal Savarkar

HarperCollins*Publishers*

Publishing operations in 17 countries and 120+ imprints globally

William Collins' dream of knowledge for all began with the publication of his first book in 1819. A self-educated mill worker, he not only enriched millions of lives, but also founded a flourishing publishing house. Today, staying true to this spirit, Collins books are packed with inspiration, innovation and practical expertise. They place you at the centre of a world of possibility and give you exactly what you need to explore it.

Published by Collins Learning
An imprint of HarperCollins*Publishers* India
Building No. 10, Tower A, 4th Floor, DLF Cyber City, Gurugram, Haryana 122002, India

First edition: 2025
Reprint: 10 9 8 7 6 5 4 3 2 1
ISBN: 978-93-6213-918-4

Artwork, typesetting and layout by **GNZE Interactions**
Printed and bound in India by Thomson Press India Ltd

ACKNOWLEDGEMENTS

Cover and title page images: Anastasiia Ovsiannykova

Inside: Title page: ChrisGorgio; **Icons:** Hiranmay Baidya, LvNL, cienpies, KaanC; **3:** impulse50; **4:** Natalia Darmoroz, impulse50, ONYXprj; **5:** Natalia Darmoroz, ONYXprj, Magnilion, colematt; **6:** Natalia Darmoroz, impulse50, ONYXprj; **8:** Natalia Darmoroz, impulse50, ONYXprj; **10:** DariuszPa, Mlenny, NAKphotos, ManOnTheGo, Thirawatana Phaisalratana; **11:** technotr, monkeybusinessimages, skynesher, Drazen_, peepo, gawrav, Kyodo News, Juan Manuel Serrano Arce; **12:** Artrise; **13:** ginosphotos, Martin Harvey, dmbaker, oleg66, xPACIFICA, ermess, domoyega, ClassicStock, Joa_Souza; **14:** carlacastagno; **15:** olgaza, FrankMirbach, Brulove, bpperry, Bulgac, stefanopolitimarkovina, Devrimb, Pavel Gerasimenko, Sepia Times; **16:** artisticco; **17:** Wolterk, viyadaistock; **18:** comotion_design; **19:** carstenbrandt, ibrandcare, Sourabh Bharti, Hindustan Times, Jeliva, Tutye, Crazybboy, NarenderSanwariya, Waradom Changyencham, Mahi Ryan; **21:** Jobalou, zak00, Smith Collection/Gado, Malachy120, Kateryna Kon/Science Photo Library, Shivendu Jauhari, Shonyjade; **22:** ivanastar, duncan1890, Whiteway; **24:** Paul Harding/Stringer, The Asahi Shimbun, Ian MacNicol; Tibrina Hobson, BSR Agency; **25:** gnagel, miralex, 2630ben, nikpal, MR1805, AmitRane1975, DKart, Sylvain CORDIER, Sarah Stier/Staff; **29:** Deshakalyan Chowdhury, Tony Russell, The India Today Group, Jack Vartoogian, Douglas Mason, Fairfax Media Archives; **30:** RachelKramer, AWM_Bonke, Kolbz, SteveAllenPhoto, rabbit75_ist, nevereverro; **31:** man_kukuku, TopVectors, kbeis, Russelltatedotcom, nicoletaionescu; **33:** Noah Seelam, Hindustan Times, Manjunath Kiran, aviation-images.com; **34:** Grafissimo, Leemage, ZU_09, traveler1116; 35: DEA / G. DAGLI ORTI, TonyBaggett, Hakat, Bettmann / Contributor, Hulton Deutsch / Contributor; **37:** Agence France Presse, Don Cravens, Tim Graham, Chris Jackson, The India Today Group, Dinodia Photos, Universal History Archive; **40:** Slaven Vlasic; **41:** CBS Photo Archive, Jeff Kravitz, Kevin Winter, CTRPhotos, Sunset Boulevard; **43:** KenCanning, VanWyckExpress, CraigRJD, 2630ben, artisteer, Nuno Tendais, FilippoBacci; **44:** STRDEL, Hindustan Times; **45:** The India Today Group, Visionhaus, seewhatmitchsee; **46:** t-lorien, dennisvdw, dangdumrong, Aroybarman, tschuma417, Freder, owngarden, MiguelAngeloSilva, Robbie Ross; **48:** ArevHamb, naveen0301; **49:** naveen0301, allou, saiko3p; **50:** Matjaz Slanic, natalie-claude, gregdh, anna1311, bonetta, kosmos111, solidcolours, Diy13; **51:** yalcinsonat1, gemenacom, Lalouetto, fstop123, JackF, 5m3photos, ISMODE, dbhanu; **52:** StephanHoerold, LdF, mevans, malerapaso, stuartbur, 123ducu; **53:** DNY59, bagi1998, Netalieh, Bozena_Fulawka, kertlis; **54:** MiklGusev, pick-uppath, Dmytro Aksonov, JHVEPhoto, Socha; **55:** melis82, shannonstent, Extreme-Photographer, tvirbickis, faracowski, vm; **56:** The India Today Group, Hindustan Times; **57:** The India Today Group, AFP, J. Countess, Hindustan Times; **60:** zhongguo, artJazz, Nick_Pandevonium, shaunl; **61:** The India Today Group, Jack Vartoogian, Subhendu Sarkar, Hindustan Times, Fairfax Media Archives, unomat; **62:** svariophoto, TracyHornbrook, mrtom-uk, scyther5, mixetto, Manuta; **63:** Bettmann; **65:** Stocktrek Images, The Asahi Shimbun, Bettmann, Historical; **66:** General Photographic Agency, brytta, sjenner13, BirdImages, antpkr, Marcin Wojciechowski, nil karaca; **67:** Satirus, Vitalii Karas, bluebay2014; **69:** subodhsathe; **70:** Heatherfaye, Print Collector, fcafotodigital, Manakin, javarman3, Hans Harms, johan10, Natalia Bogutckaia; **71:** KeithBinns, michal812; **72:** VMJones, PicturePartners, John_Kasawa, Future Publishing, Gwengoat, luoman, Leonsbox, Govindanmarudhai; **73:** LookAod; **74:** Bettmann, Stefano Bianchetti, AGF, mikroman6, Mfotophile; **75:** Indranil Mukherjee, seksan mongkhonkhamsao; **76:** doug4537, ivanastar, RelaxFoto.de, cweimer4; **77:** DmitryND, javarman3, narloch-liberra, Universal History Archive; **78:** Boyer / Contributor, Bettmann / Contributor, The Asahi Shimbun, JC Olivera; **79:** Keystone, Estate of Emil Bieber / Klaus Niermann, Mirrorpix, Simone Padovani/Awakening; **80:** AsianDream, tupungato, Pisut_Veerahong; **81:** luxiangjian4711, primeimages, pawel.gaul, Lalam; **82:** Buyenlarge, DreamStation, Hung_Chung_Chih; **83:** Culture Club, crazydiva; **84:** Martin Moos, oriredmouse, TomasSereda, Antagain, Viktorcvetkovic, ollomy, SCPixBit; **85:** elgris, KeithBinns, guenterguni, AzmanL, narvikk, Martchan, ibrandcare, Derek Brumby; **86:** Sandra Ruhaut/Contributor, Charles McQuillan/Stringer, Christian Petersen/Staff, Charles McQuillan/Stringer, Jason Koerner/Stringer, OLI SCARFF/Contributor, NARINDER NANU/Contributor; 87: Simon Bruty/Contributor, Julian Finney/Staff, ALAIN JOCARD/Contributor, Charles McQuillan/Stringer, Alex Pantling/Staff, Charles McQuillan/Stringer, Luke Hales/Staff; **88:** JMWScout, traveler1116, IndiaPictures, Waupee, aoldman, saiko3p, mazzzur, shrikant joshi; **89:** xavierarnau, ConradFries, jmoor17, ngkaki, herreid, kropic

SDG logo and icons: https://www.un.org/sustainabledevelopment/

The content of this publication has not been approved by the United Nations and does not reflect the views of the United Nations or its officials or Member States.

Browse the complete Collins catalogue at www.collins.in.
For any queries/feedback, please write to us at SCHOOLSUPPORT@harpercollins.co.in.

Preface

Like the universe, knowledge, too, is limitless. No matter how much we know, there is always more to know. In the 21st century, thanks to the leaps that technology has made and continues to make, we shall have to gather knowledge throughout our lives; so much so that we have coined a new portmanteau, to describe it: 'upskilling'.

Another novelty of the third millennium is how we access and absorb knowledge. Apart from human sources (family, teachers, friends), there are the online ones (website, social media). Yet, despite all this easy availability and accessibility, it is not always easy to distinguish between real and fake, relevant and redundant, significant and inconsequential.

Updated Knowledge Lighthouse is a series meant for GenZ, that is, learners born after Y2K. The series covers 'classic' general knowledge content for learners of grades 1 to 8, but lays special emphasis on skills —learning skills, literacy skills and life skills— as well as knowledge gleaned from new learnings of the past few years, from COVID-19 to sustainability, from data science to global issues in an ever-shifting, ever-ephemeral, post-information world. All the new chapters, although dealing with topics of great gravity, are presented in an age-appropriate and friendly manner so as to kindle interest and lay the foundation for more in-depth learning.

A critical component of the Updated Knowledge Lighthouse books is the India content, wherein our country in all its complexity and diversity is presented through colourful, simple and exciting tasks, plus brand-new features such as state-focus, city-focus and visit-a-monument.

A particularly career-friendly inclusion in the Updated Knowledge Lighthouse series is Science, technology, engineering and mathematics (STEM), the disciplines of the future, and new global issues, presented under World Today. We hope to lighten these subjects for students, by adding a little sprinkle of trivia to them.

Sustainable development is one of the key phrases of this millennium, but what does it really mean for us, especially for children? The all-new Life on Land and Climate Action chapters not only sensitise learners but also encourage direct and immediate action.

In the Skills pages, the life skills section has tasks on safety and self-awareness. Connecting the dots is the foundation of knowledge and the series has chapters based on Higher Order Thinking Skills (HOTS) and critical thinking to train young minds to see patterns, learn to eliminate or choose details and observe better.

Become a Champion Quizzer

Updated Knowledge Lighthouse encourages all learners to be curious and explore the world around them. Those who observe and absorb all the time, learn from everyone and everything; they are the ones who become quizzers. Here are six rules that will help you become a champion quizzer.

1. Be curious—look around you, see everything, read everything.
2. Listen to others.
3. Seek out new experiences.
4. Learn to link events and people.
5. Do your own research and learn to spot fake news.
6. Remember, no matter how much you know, there is much more that you have yet to learn.

Now, go for it! We are sure that this series will expose a whole new generation of learners to the fun universe of general knowledge and enhance their love for learning and discovery.

~ Seema Chari and Kunal Savarkar

In this series ...

Updated Knowledge Lighthouse tasks are thematic and linear with visual, verbal, and strategic inputs to help students solve them and acquire knowledge through a wide range of subjects and themes.

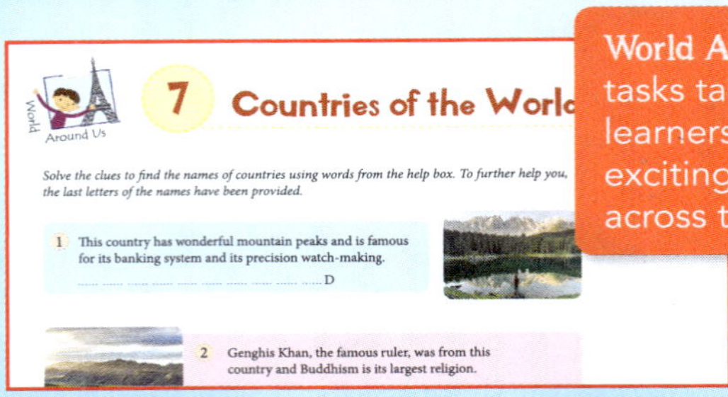

7 Countries of the World

World Around Us

Solve the clues to find the names of countries using words from the help box. To further help you, the last letters of the names have been provided.

1 This country has wonderful mountain peaks and is famous for its banking system and its precision watch-making. ....D

2 Genghis Khan, the famous ruler, was from this country and Buddhism is its largest religion.

World Around Us tasks take the learners on an exciting journey across the world.

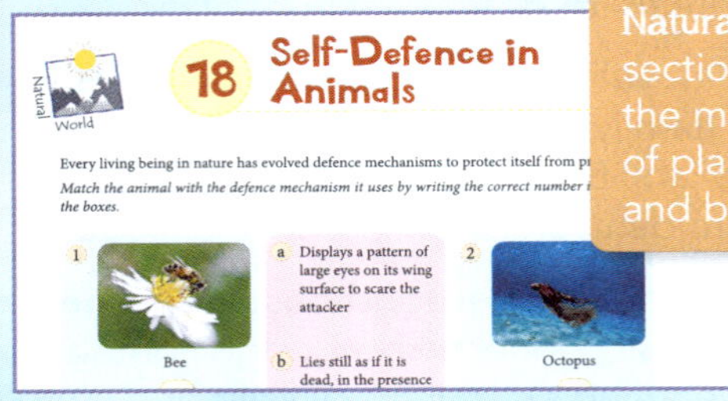

18 Self-Defence in Animals

Natural World

Every living being in nature has evolved defence mechanisms to protect itself from p...

Match the animal with the defence mechanism it uses by writing the correct number i... the boxes.

1 Bee

a Displays a pattern of large eyes on its wing surface to scare the attacker

b Lies still as if it is dead, in the presence

2 Octopus

Natural World section uncovers the magical realm of plants, animals and birds.

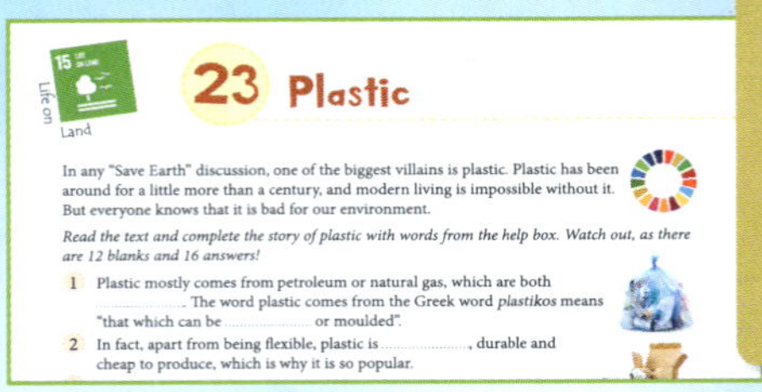

23 Plastic

Life on Land

In any "Save Earth" discussion, one of the biggest villains is plastic. Plastic has been around for a little more than a century, and modern living is impossible without it. But everyone knows that it is bad for our environment.

Read the text and complete the story of plastic with words from the help box. Watch out, as there are 12 blanks and 16 answers!

1 Plastic mostly comes from petroleum or natural gas, which are both .... The word plastic comes from the Greek word *plastikos* means "that which can be .... or moulded".

2 In fact, apart from being flexible, plastic is ...., durable and cheap to produce, which is why it is so popular.

Sustainable Development Goals sensitises learners towards sustainable development of the planet.

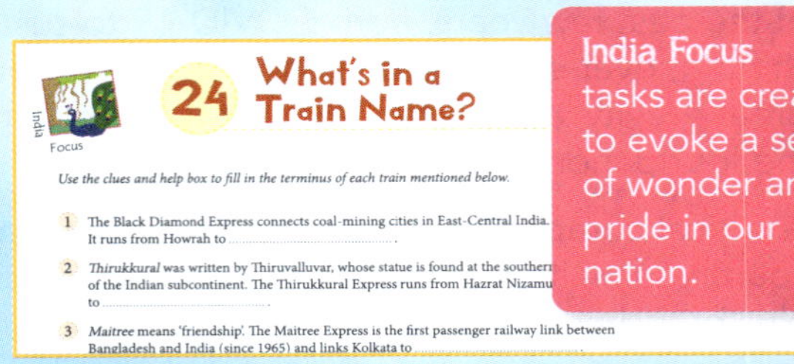

24 What's in a Train Name?

India Focus

Use the clues and help box to fill in the terminus of each train mentioned below.

1 The Black Diamond Express connects coal-mining cities in East-Central India. It runs from Howrah to ....

2 *Thirukkural* was written by Thiruvalluvar, whose statue is found at the souther... of the Indian subcontinent. The Thirukkural Express runs from Hazrat Nizamu... to ....

3 *Maitree* means 'friendship'. The Maitree Express is the first passenger railway link between Bangladesh and India (since 1965) and links Kolkata to ....

India Focus tasks are created to evoke a sense of wonder and pride in our nation.

34 That's My Music!

Art and Entertainment

When you enjoy the music of an artist or band, you try to listen to everything they've created.

Match each set of songs with the musician or band.

1 *Roar*
Chained to the Rhythm
Firework

2 *Gorgeous*
You Belong With Me
Blank Space

a Justin Bieber

b Demi Lovato

Art and Entertainment tasks celebrate artists, artworks, paintings, movies, awards and achievements.

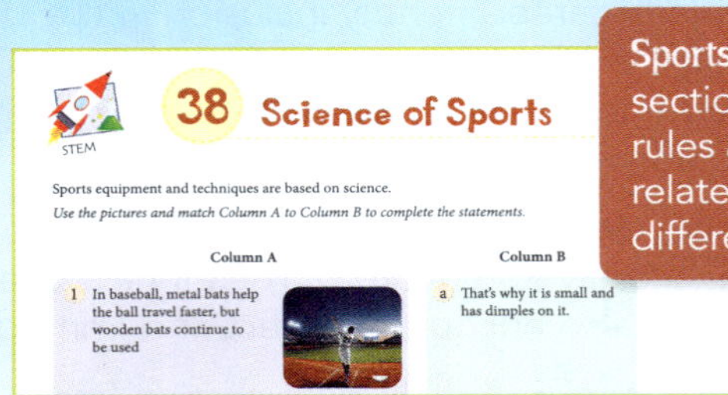

38 Science of Sports

STEM

Sports equipment and techniques are based on science.

Use the pictures and match Column A to Column B to complete the statements.

Column A	Column B
1 In baseball, metal bats help the ball travel faster, but wooden bats continue to be used	a That's why it is small and has dimples on it.

Sports section provides rules and records related to different sports.

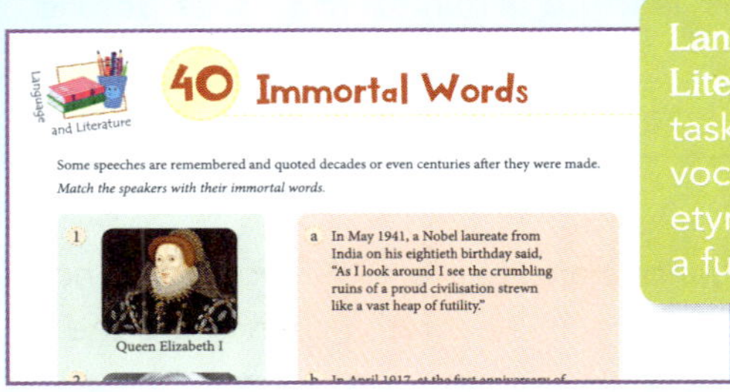

40 Immortal Words

Language and Literature

Some speeches are remembered and quoted decades or even centuries after they were made.

Match the speakers with their immortal words.

1 Queen Elizabeth I

a In May 1941, a Nobel laureate from India on his eightieth birthday said, "As I look around I see the crumbling ruins of a proud civilisation strewn like a vast heap of futility."

Language and Literature tasks present vocabulary and etymology in a fun way.

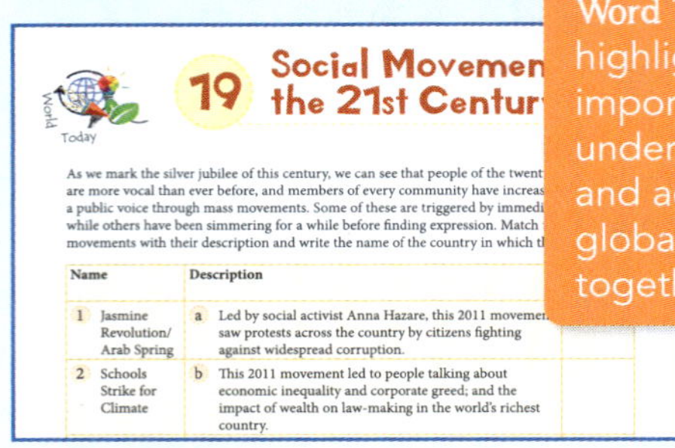

19 Social Movemen... the 21st Centur...

World Today

As we mark the silver jubilee of this century, we can see that people of the twent... are more vocal than ever before, and members of every community have increas... a public voice through mass movements. Some of these are triggered by immedi... while others have been simmering for a while before finding expression. Match... movements with their description and write the name of the country in which t...

Name	Description
1 Jasmine Revolution/ Arab Spring	a Led by social activist Anna Hazare, this 2011 movemen... saw protests across the country by citizens fighting against widespread corruption.
2 Schools Strike for Climate	b This 2011 movement led to people talking about economic inequality and corporate greed; and the impact of wealth on law-making in the world's richest country.

Word Today highlights the importance of understanding and addressing global challenges together.

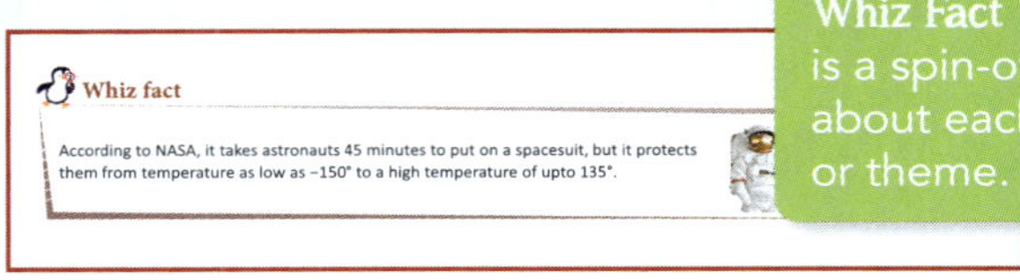

Whiz fact

According to NASA, it takes astronauts 45 minutes to put on a spacesuit, but it protects them from temperature as low as –150° to a high temperature of upto 135°.

Whiz Fact is a spin-off fact about each topic or theme.

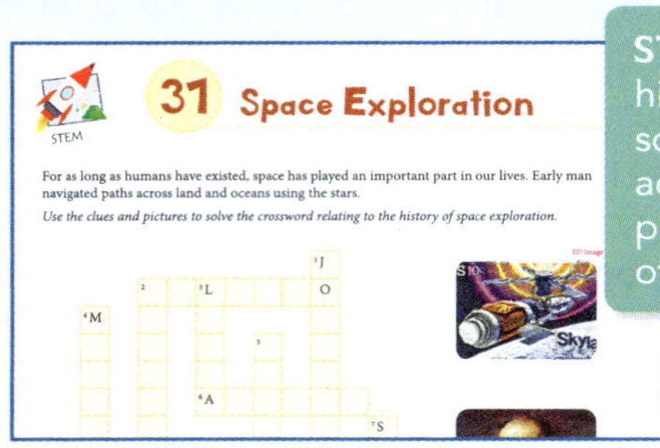

31 Space Exploration

STEM

For as long as humans have existed, space has played an important part in our lives. Early man navigated paths across land and oceans using the stars.

Use the clues and pictures to solve the crossword relating to the history of space exploration.

STEM highlights some scientific achievements and provides facts for others.

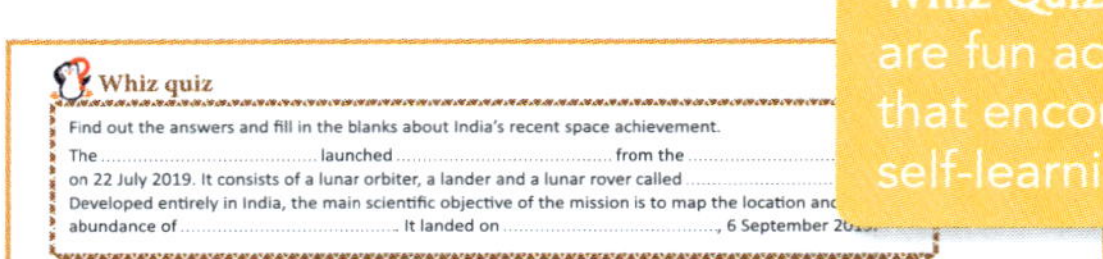

Whiz quiz

Find out the answers and fill in the blanks about India's recent space achievement.

The .... launched .... from the .... on 22 July 2019. It consists of a lunar orbiter, a lander and a lunar rover called .... Developed entirely in India, the main scientific objective of the mission is to map the location and abundance of .... It landed on ...., 6 September 20...

Whiz Quiz are fun activities that encourage self-learning.

21st Century Skills

21st century skills are necessary to succeed in the Age of Information. These skills are divided into three main sets, namely, learning skills, literacy skills and life skills.

Learning Skills

- Critical Thinking and HOTS
- Creativity
- Collaboration
- Communication

Learning Skills

14 Startups Around Us

In the last 20 years or so, new companies, popularly known as startups, have used technology to change the way we live, travel, eat and shop.

Use the fun clues to get the names of 11 such brands and solve the crossword below.

Literacy Skills

- Technology
- Information
- Media
- Financial Literacy
- Data Handling

Literacy Skills

57 The Printing Press

Before the invention of the printing press, books were produced by hand. They were written on clay, parchment wax or papyrus. Each book had to be painstakingly copied by hand to make another copy of it—till the invention of the printing press by Johannes Gutenberg between 1440 and 1450.
The very first book he printed on the press was the *Bible*, prized today as the *Gutenberg Bible*.

1 Between 1300s and 1400s, people used a very basic form of printing using wooden stamps. In this form of printing, letters or images are cut on blocks of wood, which are dipped in ink and then stamped onto paper.

2 Gutenberg realised that he could use cut blocks within a machine to make the printing process a lot quicker.

3 Gutenberg replaced wood blocks with metal block letters, which

Life Skills

- Problem-solving
- Self-awareness
- Safety
- Social Skills

Life Skills

22 Safety in the Cyber World

The Internet is a great place to know more about things we don't know and to keep in touch with our friends and family. But it also has dangers and threats that we should know about.

Match the clues in Column A with those in Column B to show that you know how to be safe online.

Column A	Column B
1 Sites that have HTTPS in the address bar	a log out of all websites you've accessed and close all the windows you've opened before leaving the computer.
2 When working on a public computer, always	b are safer than sites that have HTTP.
3 Never share your passwords	c without scanning it using an antivirus program.
4 Even if a bank employee calls or emails you,	d unless you have the copyright to do so.
5 Unless you are thirteen years or older	e do not share your login details with them.

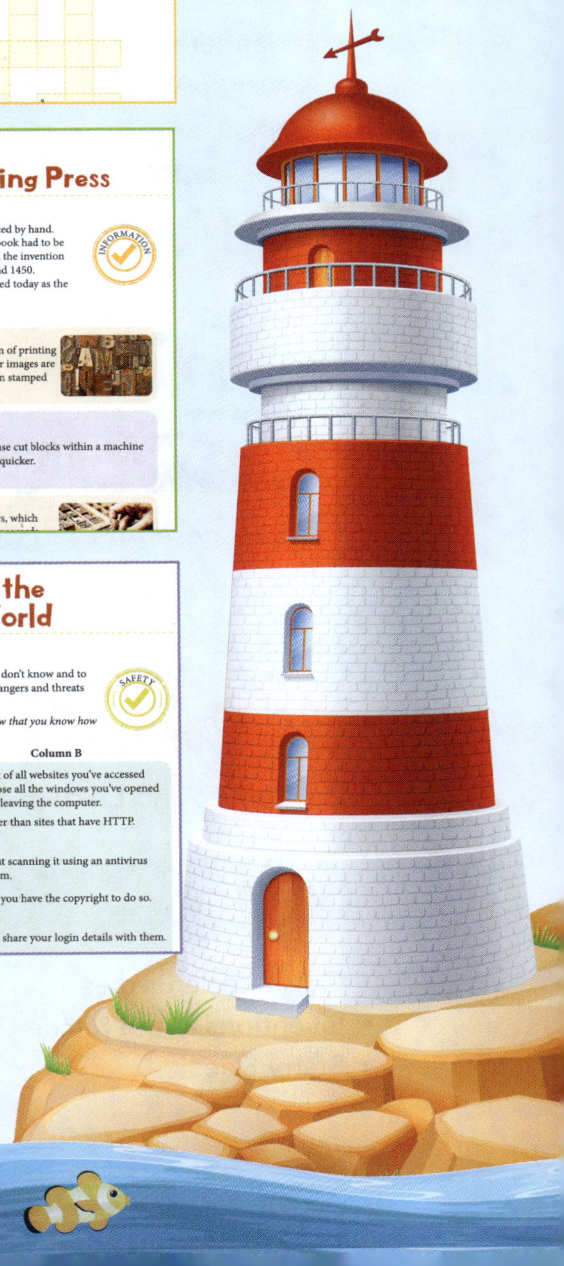

Detailed Contents

World Around Us

- Rivers and Capitals
- Get Your Dancing Shoes On!
- Statuesque!
- Travelling to a Place Unknown
- Social Reformers
- Languages Across Countries
- Tribes of the World
- Madagascar!
- Scandinavia
- One and Only
- Bridge Structures

Natural World

- Endangered Animals
- Amazing Animal Traits
- Primates
- Natural Disasters

Language and Literature

- Homophones
- Unforgettable Characters
- Confront Your Fears
- British and American English

Art and Entertainment

- Japanese Arts and Crafts
- Space Films

World Today

- Pandemics and Epidemics

STEM

- Our Miracle Bodies
- Inventions in the Kitchen
- Starry Skies
- Science Shockers
- Scientific Breakthroughs

India Focus

- Abbreviations
- Parks and Sanctuaries
- Great Musicians of India
- Touch the Sky with Glory
- And The Award Is...
- Mayanagari Mumbai
- India's First Women
- Indian String Instruments
- Constitution of India
- GI-tagged Products
- Indian Nobel Laureates
- Victoria Memorial
- India Tourism

Sports

- National Sports
- Olympic All-time Greats
- Extreme Sports
- India at the Paris Olympics

Sustainable Development Goals

- Pollution Alert!
- Plogging Away
- Energy Sources
- Measures to Reduce Pollution

Learning Skills

- Pattern Recognition
- Reversible or Irreversible?

Literacy Skills

- Stamped!
- Tech-wiz
- How The Car Came To Be

Life Skills

- Etiquette at the Mall
- Measuring Tools

Contents

1	Abbreviations	9
2	Rivers and Capitals	10
3	National Sports	11
4	Homophones	12
5	Get Your Dancing Shoes On!	13
6	Pattern Recognition	14
7	Japanese Arts and Crafts	15
8	Etiquette at the Mall	16
9	Our Miracle Bodies	18
10	Parks and Sanctuaries	19
11	Reversible or Irreversible?	20
12	Pandemics and Epidemics	21
13	Unforgettable Characters	22
14	Olympic All-time Greats	24
15	Endangered Animals	26
16	Inventions in the Kitchen	28
17	Great Musicians of India	29
18	Statuesque!	30
19	Confront Your Fears	31
20	Pollution Alert!	32
21	Touch the Sky with Glory	33
22	Travelling to a Place Unknown	34
23	Starry Skies	36
24	Social Reformers	37
25	Plogging Away	38
26	Languages Across Countries	39
27	Space Films	40
28	Amazing Animal Traits	42
29	And The Award Is...	44
30	Primates	46
31	Mayanagari Mumbai	48
32	British and American English	50
33	Measuring Tools	52
34	Extreme Sports	54
35	India's First Women	56
36	Stamped!	58
37	Energy Sources	60
38	Indian String Instruments	61
39	Tech-wiz	62
40	Science Shockers	64
41	Natural Disasters	65
42	Tribes of the World	66
43	Scientific Breakthroughs	67
44	Constitution of India	68
45	Madagascar!	70
46	GI-tagged Products	72
47	How The Car Came To Be	74
48	Scandinavia	76
49	Indian Nobel Laureates	78
50	Measures to Reduce Pollution	80
51	Victoria Memorial	82
52	One and Only	84
53	India at the Paris Olympics	86
54	India Tourism	88
55	Bridge Structures	89
	Quiz Yourself 1	90
	Quiz Yourself 2	91
	Quiz Yourself 3	92
	Quiz Yourself 4	93
	Answer Key	94

India Focus

1 Abbreviations

An abbreviation is a shortened form of a word or phrase. For instance, Mr and Mrs are popular abbreviations for Mister and Missus. Places can also have abbreviations.

Match the given abbreviations used for vehicle registrations with the names of their states or union territories of India.

	Abbreviation
1	CG
2	ML
3	MZ
4	KA
5	LD
6	SK
7	TR
8	DD
9	GA
10	MH

	State/UT
a	Tripura
b	Lakshadweep
c	Chhattisgarh
d	Maharashtra
e	Dadra and Nagar Haveli and Daman and Diu
f	Goa
g	Meghalaya
h	Karnataka
i	Mizoram
j	Sikkim

Whiz fact

The Government of India has introduced a new system of issuing registration plates for cars. The BH series (short for Bharat) can be issued to private cars owned by employees of defence or central/state government offices as well as those working in PSUs or private firms with offices in four or more states. This system prevents the need for giving up the registration plate of a particular state and applying for a new one upon being transferred from one state to another.

2 Rivers and Capitals

Many of the world's cities have rivers running through them. This is because in the olden days, water was an important means of transportation which connected places to one another.

Given below are the names of some rivers and the first part of the names of capital cities through which the rivers run. Choose one fragment from the help box to add to the letters to find the name of the capital city. Then add the name of the country in which the city is located.

	Rivers	Letters of the Capital Cities	Countries
1	Tagus	LIS + ...	....
2	Tigris	BAGH + ...	....
3	Chao Praya	BANG + ...	....
4	Han	SEO + ...	....
5	Manzanares	MAD + ...	....
6	Vistula	WAR + ...	....
7	Pasig	MAN + ...	....
8	Taedong	PYONG + ...	....
9	Sava	BELG + ...	....
10	Barada	DAMAS + ...	....

Help box

YANG RID BON CUS RADE

UL DAD KOK SAW ILA

3 National Sports

Use the pictures and the names in the help box to identify the national sports of these countries. But watch out! There are some extra sports in the help box.

1 

Japan

....

2 

Bangladesh

....

3 

South Korea

....

4 

Spain

....

5 

United States of America

....

6 

Austria

....

7 

Scotland

....

8 

Sri Lanka

....

Help box

Wrestling | Bullfighting | Golf | Kalaripayattu | Sumo wrestling | Baseball | Football | Hockey | Alpine skiing | Taekwondo | Kabaddi | Ice hockey | Volleyball

Whiz fact

Canada and Estonia have two national sports, depending on the season. Canada's national summer sport is lacrosse and Estonia's national summer sport is basketball. Ice hockey is the national winter sport of both these countries.

4 Homophones

Homophones are words which sound or are spelled the same, but mean different things.

Choose the correct word from each pair of homophones so that the sentence makes sense.

1. My parents always took the rode/road that passed the zoo and the library.
2. Here's a sign that asks us to look out for deer/dear while crossing the road.
3. I believe the rich man had no air/heir, so he left his money to a charity.
4. The thief stole the purse from right under the woman's nose/knows.
5. It will take one week/weak to complete this project.
6. The teacher asked them to write/right their answers clearly.
7. We usually eat our cereal/serial in steal/steel bowls.
8. Anyone who ascended the throne/thrown after the old King's death would/wood have to wear purple robes for the rest of their life.
9. Have you read/red the rules of the competition?
10. People said the school won many awards because the Principle/Principal was very strict.
11. Could I please have a piece/peace of chocolate?
12. If I could climb only one/won mountain peek/peak, it would be Mount Kilimanjaro.
13. The GPS shows a heard/herd of cattle blocking this road.
14. I'm going to the store to bye/buy some blew/blue cheese and a loaf of bread/bred.
15. The autorickshaw driver was not willing to charge the correct fair/fare.
16. What can you buy for sixteen sense/cents?

Whiz fact

Sometimes, homophones come in sets of threes. For instance, there, their and they're, and to, two and too. Can you think of any others?

World Around Us

5 Get Your Dancing Shoes On!

Dancing is a great way to express and enjoy oneself and get some exercise done.

Use the images and the help box to identify the popular dances in these countries.

1 

Brazil

....

2 

China

....

3 

South Africa

....

4 

Czech Republic

....

5 

Argentina

....

6 

Russia

....

7 

Spain

....

8 

United States

....

Help box

Polka	Ballet	Samba	Flamenco
Tango	Dragon dance	Hip-hop	Zulu dance

Whiz fact

The tarantella is either a graceful courtship dance or a magico-religious solo dance that was once believed to be performed by a person bitten by the venomous spider, tarantula, presumably under delirium!

Learning Skills

6 Pattern Recognition

All of us use patterns to learn and to act. Recognising a face, knowing the traffic rules, how to behave, being alert to danger, all of these, in fact, every facet of life depends upon our ability to recognise patterns.

COMMUNICATION

Here is some apparently nonsense text, with the words all misspelled. But you should be able to read it. Write the text correctly in the lines provided and discuss with your classmates how you could read this text.

I cnduo't bvleiee taht I culod aulaclty uesdtannrd waht I was rdnaieg. Unisg the icndeblire pweor of the hmuan mnid, aocdcrnig to a rseecrah at Cmabrigde Uinervtisy, it dseno't mttaer in waht oderr the lterets in a wrod are, the olny irpoamtnt tihng is taht the frsit and lsat ltteer be in the rhgit pclae. The rset can be a taotl mses and you can sitll raed it whoutit a pboerlm. Tihs is bucseae the huamn mnid deos not raed ervey ltteer by istlef, but the wrod as a wlohe. Aaznmig, huh? Yaeh and I awlyas tghhuot slelinpg was ipmorantt!

See if yuor fdreins can raed tihs too.

Whiz fact

The inability to read correctly is called dyslexia, while the inability to write correctly is a condition called dysgraphia.

Art and Entertainment

7 Japanese Arts and Crafts

Japan's unique artistic traditions and techniques have led to many prized arts and crafts.

Write the correct number in each box to match the description of each craft with the correct image.

1 

2 

3 

4 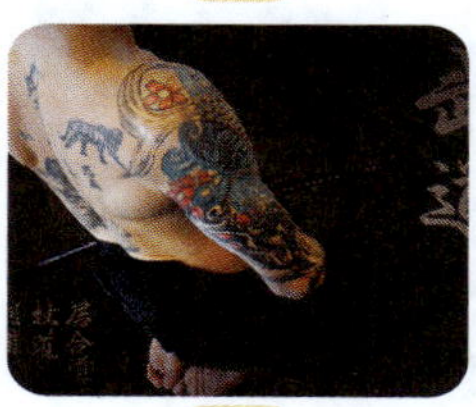

a Shodo is the highly stylised art of Japanese calligraphy created with a brush.

b Manga are Japanese comic books that represent a vibrant form of art and writing.

c Origami is the Japanese art of folding paper to create decorative art.

d Maki-e is a type of Japanese lacquerware decorated with powdered silver and gold.

e Amigurumi is the Japanese craft of knitting or crocheting small animals or creatures.

f Irezumi is the Japanese tradition of tattooing.

g Ikebana is the Japanese art of flower arrangement.

h Bonsai is the Japanese art of growing very small shrubs and trees in pots.

5 

6 

7 

8 

Whiz fact

Kirigami literally means 'cut paper'. It is like origami, except more elaborate designs are cut out of paper.

Life Skills

8 Etiquette at the Mall

SOCIAL SKILLS

Malls are springing up everywhere and they are popular places to hang out. They are clean, well-lit, temperature-controlled and offer places to sit, eat and shop.

Tick (✓) the actions that show correct etiquette at a mall.

1 At the mall,

a make the most of your time in the common areas even if you talk and laugh a bit loudly with your friends. After all, you have come to have a good time. ☐

b be mindful that you are sharing the space with many others who might be disturbed by the noise you make. ☐

2 As you wait for your friend to join you,

a stand away from entrances, exits to stairs, escalators, stairways and stores. ☐

b decide to meet at the escalator, lift or the doorway of a store as it is easy to spot these places from a distance. ☐

3 At the food court,

a load up on extra cutlery and condiments. You can carry them home and use them later. ☐

b help yourself only to cutlery and condiments that you will use. Anything more is dishonest and wasteful of the environment. ☐

4 If some of your friends are a bit away from you on the escalator,

a stay where you are. You can catch up with them when you get off it.

b excuse yourself, push through other shoppers and climb towards your friends.

5 When you use the bathroom,

a leave the toilet clean for the next person to use.

b use as much toilet paper as you want and litter as there are people employed to clean up.

6 If there are many people waiting to use the toilet,

a get in line and wait for your turn.

b say sorry and push your way through into the first vacant stall you can find.

7 If someone who doesn't have a phone gets separated from you,

a split up and shout their name in each corridor so that they know you are looking for them.

b go to the information help desk and ask them to make an announcement so the person can meet you there.

8 An area of the atrium has been cordoned off because of maintenance work and you need to take a long detour to get to the other side of the mall,

a just duck under the yellow or red tape and carefully make your way across.

b take the long route as you don't know what dangers you may be courting if you don't take the detour.

Whiz fact

Nine of the biggest ten malls in the world are in Asia, of which the biggest is in Tehran, Iran. They have between 500 and 2500 stores each. The Mall of America in Bloomington, Minnesota, USA is the only one outside Asia.

9 Our Miracle Bodies

STEM

The human body is a miracle of flesh, bones and blood. Scientists are still trying to understand how the human body performs its various functions.

Tick (✓) the word that makes each sentence true.

1. The largest bone in the human body is the femur/rib. It can support 30 times the weight of a person's body.
2. The heart/liver is the largest internal organ in the human body and the only one capable of regenerating itself.
3. The skin is thickest on your eyelids/palms and soles.
4. The fastest muscles in the body are the ones that make the eyes blink/make you sneeze.
5. Routine shedding of layers of tissues of intestine/stomach maintains optimal health.
6. Bones/Teeth are the only part of the human body that cannot heal and repair on their own.
7. One-fourth of all the bones in the human body are found in the feet/ribs.

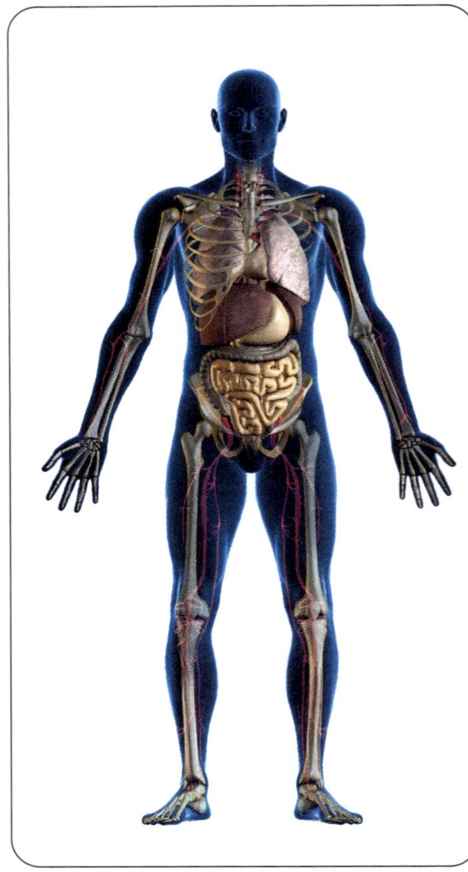

Whiz quiz

Write the name of the body part that never grows. ....

Whiz fact

The word 'organ' comes from an ancient Greek word *organon*, which means 'tool' or 'instrument'.

India Focus

10 Parks and Sanctuaries

India has many national parks and wildlife sanctuaries that host different types of birds and animals.

Fill in the blanks with the correct words from the help box.

1. The .... National Park and Wildlife Sanctuary is where the Asiatic lion can be spotted.

2. The rare Kashmir red stag or hangul can be seen at the .... National Park.
3. The rare endangered mountain goat called the Nilgiri Tahr is found in the .... National Park.
4. The Bharatpur Bird Sanctuary is now formally called the .... National Park where migratory birds can be found.
5. The endangered snow leopard can be spotted at the .... National Park.

6. The .... Wildlife Sanctuary shelters the rare Indian bison.

7. The endangered one-horned rhino has the .... National Park as its sanctuary.
8. The Bengal tiger is one of the animals you can find at the .... National Park.

Help box

Sundarbans | Keoladeo | Chinnar | Kaziranga | Gir | Hemis | Eravikulam | Dachigam

Whiz fact

There are over fifty tiger reserves in India. Some of them are Manas National Park in Assam, Jim Corbett National Park in Uttarakhand and Anamalai Tiger Reserve in Tamil Nadu.

Learning Skills

11 Reversible or Irreversible?

You know that things can be solid, liquid or gas. Some things change from solid to liquid, for instance, ice melts to water. They may also change from liquid to solid, for instance, water freezing to ice. These are reversible changes.

An egg cracking is not reversible, because we cannot put an egg back in its shell and make it whole again. These are called irreversible changes. Rusting of iron and digestion of food are both irreversible changes because the original iron and food cannot be retrieved.

CRITICAL THINKING

Write which changes are reversible and which are irreversible and give reasons why.

1. Baking a cake ....
2. Bursting of crackers ....

3. Mixing salt in water ....
4. Grinding wood into sawdust ....

5. Milk turning sour ....
6. Shredding paper ....

7. Breaking a toy ....

8. Burning of coal ....
9. Crushing a plastic bottle ....

10. Making a copper wire from a sheet of copper ....
11. Breaking glass ....

12. Crumpling a paper bag ....

Whiz fact

Dry ice, the ice used to keep ice cream in carts cold, is solidified carbon dioxide. It evaporates directly into the air without turning into liquid. When carbon dioxide has to be turned into dry ice, it is first converted to liquid form.

World Today

12 Pandemics and Epidemics

COVID-19 is not the first pandemic that the world has seen. Here is a list of pandemics and epidemics through the ages.

Rearrange the jumbled letters to write the names of the diseases that caused each of them.

Images	Pandemics	Jumbled Clue	Answer
1 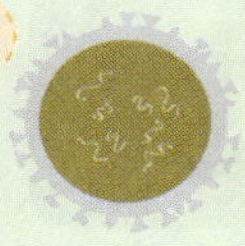	In 1918–19, a pandemic named 'The Spanish flu' spread across the world, affecting millions, and then suddenly disappeared!	AZNELFUNI	
2 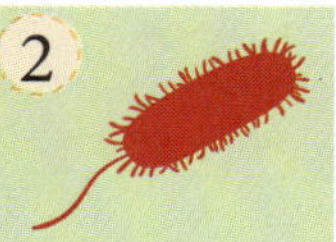	This terrible disease has caused no less than 7 pandemics. It occurs when a certain kind of bacteria infects food and water.	ARELOCH	
3 	Millions of people worldwide can get infected with this epidemic disease that is spread by mosquitoes.	ARAMALI	
4 	For centuries, this was the worst pandemic ever seen by humans. It was called the 'Black Death' in Europe.	GULAPE	
5 	The first case of this deadly disease was only recorded in 1981 but it has spread across the world. It is a world epidemic.	SIDA	
6 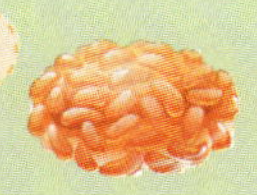	This deadly disease gave rise to many epidemics across the world. Those who survived it remained badly scarred.	LALMSOPX	
7 	This disease was called 'camp fever' or 'jail fever' because it seemed to affect soldiers and prisoners much more.	SHUTPY	
8 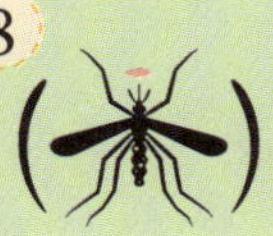	Also caused by mosquitoes, this disease has caused dozens of epidemics over the past few centuries.	WOLYEL REVEF	

Whiz fact

To this day, smallpox is the only human infectious disease that has been completely removed or eradicated. So, nobody in the world will die of it ever again.

Language and Literature

13 Unforgettable Characters

All our favourite books are filled with unforgettable characters.

Match the characters with the books they're from.

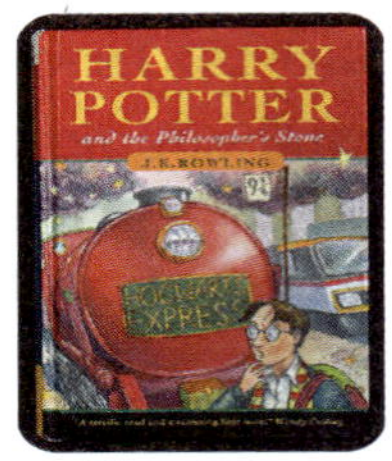

Characters

1. A talking lion named Aslan
2. A girl called Dorothy who travelled with her companions, the Tin Man, the Scarecrow and the Lion
3. A teddy bear whose best friend is a pig
4. An orphan girl who goes to the land of giants and later meets the Queen of England
5. A bear from Darkest Peru who goes to London
6. An orphaned boy who lives with his uncle and aunt before going to school to learn magic
7. A fierce beast who will die when the last petal of an enchanted rose falls off, unless he can find true love before that
8. This housekeeper repeatedly misunderstands what people ask her to do because she takes everything literally

Books

a. *Winnie-the-Pooh*

b. *The Lion, the Witch and the Wardrobe*

c. *A Bear called Paddington*

d. *Beauty and the Beast*

e. *The Wonderful Wizard of Oz*

f. *Amelia Bedelia*

g. *The BFG*

h. *Harry Potter and the Philosopher's Stone*

9	A boy who was raised in a wolf pack in a jungle	i	*Noddy and his Car*
10	A mouse who lives with his human parents and brother	j	*Peter Pan*
11	A girl named Katniss who has to use her skills at archery to defeat other contestants to win a competition	k	*Charlie and the Chocolate Factory*
12	A strange man named Mr Willy Wonka who holds a competition to let children visit his factory	l	*Sweet Valley Twins*
13	Wendy and a fairy called Tinkerbell are friends with a boy who can fly	m	*The Hunger Games*
14	A wooden toy who lives in Toyland with his friend, Big Ears	n	*Alice's Adventures in Wonderland*
15	Jessica and Elizabeth are the Sweet Valley twins, very different from each other	o	*Stuart Little*
16	This girl tumbles down a rabbit hole and has adventures with the Mad Hatter, the March Hare and Queen of Hearts, among other strange characters	p	*The Jungle Book*

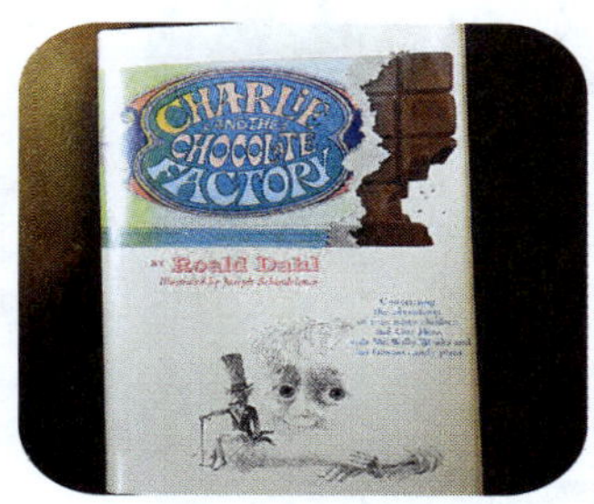

Whiz fact

The *Little House* books are a series of books by Laura Ingalls Wilder. The books show how people lived in those times. In those days, a school had all its children sitting in one room and there was only one teacher who taught them everything!

Sports

14 Olympic All-time Greats

Winning an Olympic medal is one way of feeling on top of the world. There are some all-time greats who have won multiple Olympic medals.

Identify the sports for which these sportspersons have won medals using words from the help box.

1 Paavo Nurmi of Finland, nicknamed the 'Flying Finn', dominated the world of distance running in the 1920s, winning 9 golds and 3 silvers. ....

2 British rower Steve Redgrave won an Olympic Gold from the 1984 Los Angeles Games to the 2000 Sydney Olympics, but not in the same event. ....

3 Larisa Latynina of the erstwhile Soviet Union won 9 gold, 5 silver and 4 bronze medals, giving her the second-highest number of Olympic medals in the world. ....

4 With 23 gold, 3 silver and 2 bronze medals, Michael Phelps of the United States leads the Olympic medal tally with a heart-stopping 28 medals. ....

5 Italian Edoardo Mangiarotti won 6 gold, 5 silver and 2 bronze medals for a total tally of 13 Olympic medals. ....

6 Usain Bolt of Jamaica won 9 Olympic gold medals, of which he lost one because a team-mate tested positive for drug use. ....

7 Cuban wrestler Mijain Lopez became the first to win 5 gold medals in the same individual event. He has now won the men's 130-kg Greco-Roman event from the 2008 Olympics to the 2024 Paris Olympics. ....

8 Birgit Fischer won 8 gold and 4 silver medals at the Olympics, some representing East Germany, others representing Germany. ....

9 Isabell Werth of Germany won 6 gold and 4 silver Olympic medals. ....

10 Carl Lewis of the United States won 9 gold and 1 silver at the Olympics. ....

11 Ireen Wüst of Netherlands won 11 medals at the Olympics, 5 gold, 5 silver and 1 bronze. ....

Help box

Swimming | Wrestling | Sprinting | Speed skating | Dressage | Cross country
Athletics | Fencing | Kayaking | Rowing | Gymnastics

Whiz fact

During the first modern Olympics in 1896, first-place winners were crowned with an olive wreath and awarded a silver medal. It was not until the 1904 Summer Olympics that the now-famous gold, silver and bronze medals were awarded.

15 Endangered Animals

Animals become endangered because they are hunted, because of their habitat loss and due to climate change that affects their sources of food.

Solve the crossword to identify some endangered animals with the help of pictures and clues.

1 

2 

3 

4 

5 

6 

7 

8 

9 

10 

11 

Across

1 Also known as the Asiatic wild dog, it is found in mountainous regions of Southeast Asia, India and China, and is nearly untameable.

3 Its name means 'person of the forest' and it lives on the islands of Borneo and Sumatra.

5 A fish-eating crocodile found in the northern part of the Indian subcontinent.

7 Found in North America, it threatened livestock, so it was hunted, trapped and poisoned to the point that it is now endangered.

Down

2 The world's largest lizard, it exists on five small Indonesian islands.

4 The only parrot incapable of flight, it has whiskers under its beak and is found in New Zealand.

6 The largest animal on the planet is no longer hunted but is threatened by climate change which affects its main source of food.

8 Arboreal primates that are found only in the jungles of Southeast Asia.

9 Found in India, Bangladesh, Bhutan and Nepal, poaching and habitat loss are responsible for it being declared endangered.

10 This animal lives in the Andalusia region of Spain and is endangered because of loss of habitat, loss of prey and diseases.

11 This is the most trafficked animal in the world, hunted for its scales.

Help box

Mexican wolf | Tarsier | Bengal tiger | Komodo dragon | Dhole | Kakapo
Pangolin | Iberian lynx | Gharial | Orangutan | Blue whale

Whiz fact

The thylacine, also known as the Tasmanian tiger, is now considered extinct. The largest carnivorous marsupial of modern times, the thylacine was native to Australia, New Guinea and particularly Tasmania, its last known range.

STEM

16 Inventions in the Kitchen

Many useful kitchen appliances have made life convenient for us.

Read the clues to find the names of the inventions hidden in the grid.

B	R	A	H	B	Z	E	I	G	E	R	N
K	E	T	T	L	E	S	C	H	W	Z	E
S	S	C	F	E	C	X	Z	P	O	I	V
A	T	L	R	N	A	I	A	U	I	A	O
L	R	U	V	D	Z	X	C	V	B	Q	E
F	X	M	B	E	T	R	T	R	Y	M	V
S	C	B	E	R	S	P	L	I	N	T	A
O	S	R	E	E	A	Q	C	X	U	I	W
M	E	Y	P	T	U	E	E	A	Q	X	O
R	O	T	A	R	E	G	I	R	F	E	R
E	R	L	S	T	R	V	A	W	A	C	C
H	G	A	S	S	T	O	V	E	E	A	I
T	M	N	K	L	Q	S	P	O	A	U	M

1. This jar with a rotating metal blade at the bottom grinds food into a paste form and was invented by Stephen Poplawski in 1922.
2. In 1947, Percy Spencer invented this appliance that is used to heat and cook food.
3. Sir James Dewar invented this gadget in 1892 to keep liquids hot or cold.
4. This device that uses electricity to heat water was invented by Arthur Leslie Large in 1922.
5. In 1805, Oliver Evans designed the first machine which used not water but vapour to cool products.
6. The surface on which we cook food today was invented by Sir Benjamin Thompson in the United States in 1790. The flaw in this invention was fixed by Englishman James Sharp in 1826.

Whiz fact

The toaster was invented by Scotsman Alan MacMasters in 1893, but toasting bread was a common activity even in the Roman times. It was done to prolong the shelf life of bread. In fact, *tostus* is the Latin word for scorching or burning.

India Focus

17 Great Musicians of India

These are images of musicians playing their instruments.

Group them based on which musicians play the same instrument.

G S Sachdev

Ustad Amjad Ali Khan

Nikhil Banerjee

Zakir Hussain

Tabla

1 ...., ...

Sitar

2 ...., ...

Sarod

3 ...., ...

Bansuri

4 ...., ...

Kishan Maharaj

Hariprasad Chaurasia

Ali Akbar Khan

Ravi Shankar

Whiz fact

Ustad Bismillah Khan, a renowned *shehnai* player, was awarded all four of India's civilian honours: the Padma Shri, the Padma Bhushan, the Padma Vibhushan and the Bharat Ratna.

18 Statuesque!

The cultural riches of our ancestors are clearly visible in the incredible range and geographical spread of statues they created.

Match the descriptions to the images of the statues.

1 The *Pietà*, made by Michelangelo, depicts the body of the crucified Jesus on the lap of his mother, Mary. It is housed in St Peter's Basilica in the Vatican City.

2 The *Terrace of the Lions of Delos* in Greece is a row of 12 stone lions facing east towards the sacred lake of Delos.

3 The *Giant Buddha of Leshan* in China is carved out of rock. The gaze of the Buddha was supposed to calm the turbulent waters of the rivers Min and Dadu so that shipping vessels could ply.

4 The *Moai* are massive human figures made of stone with overly large heads in Easter Island, Chile. They are carved from the volcanic crater Rano Raraku and were built to honour deified ancestors.

5 The statue of Christ the Redeemer overlooks the city of Rio de Janeiro in Brazil. It is a symbol of Christianity all over the world.

6 The *Little Mermaid* immortalises the fairy tale of the same name. The bronze statue is by the waterside in Copenhagen, Denmark.

a

b

c

d

e

f

Whiz fact

The Buddhas of Bamyan were two monumental statues of Buddha carved into the side of a cliff in Bamyan, Afghanistan. They were 35 metres and 53 metres tall respectively. They were destroyed by the Taliban in 2001.

Language and Literature

19 Confront Your Fears

Everyone is afraid of something, but there are some really strange things that people can be afraid of.

Pick the correct word from the help box to make each statement true. Use the clue given in brackets after each sentence.

1 .... phobia is the fear of water. (aquatic)

2 .... phobia is the fear of paper. (papyrus)

3 .... phobia is the fear of the number 8. (octagon)

4 .... phobia is the fear of being alone. (autistic)

5 .... phobia is the fear of heights. (acrobat)

6 .... phobia is the fear of numbers. (arithmetic)

7 .... phobia is the fear of the night. (noctural)

8 .... phobia is the fear of horses. (equestrian)

9 .... phobia is the fear of sleep. (insomnia)

10 .... phobia is the fear of colours. (chromatic)

11 .... phobia is the fear of school. (scholastic)

12 .... phobia is the fear of large things. (megalithic)

Help box

Megalo	Acro	Arithmo	Equino	Papyro	Octo
Somni	Aqua	Scoliono	Nocti	Chromo	Auto

Whiz fact

Trypanophobia is the fear of injections, cynophobia is the fear of dogs and triskaidekaphobia is fear of the number 13. Then there's the fear of love, called philophobia!

13 CLIMATE ACTION

Climate Action

20 Pollution Alert!

There are many different types of pollution that impact human health and the future of life on Earth—air, water, soil, noise and light pollution.

Given below are statements about pollution. Say whether they are true or false by writing T or F against each one.

1. Soil pollution reduces the fertility of farms so that each unit of land has less production and lower quality crops.
2. Wearing masks is one way of reducing the number and kind of air pollutants that enter the human body.
3. Noise pollution causes deafness, tiredness and stress-induced diseases.
4. Human beings are not able to enjoy restful sleep because of light pollution.
5. Oceans do not have any water pollution.
6. Planting trees reduces soil pollution because the roots hold the soil in place.
7. Using renewable sources of energy such as solar and wind power are excellent ways of reducing pollution.
8. Factories often release harmful metals and chemicals into rivers, harming the fish and soil.
9. Using headphones reduces noise pollution.
10. Using public transportation does not make any difference to the levels of air pollution.
11. When water is polluted, even the crops irrigated with that water are likely to be polluted.

Whiz fact

Of the 15 most polluted cities in the world, 10 are in India. India also holds the dubious distinction of having 63 of the top 100 most polluted cities in the world. We need to take urgent steps to reduce the pollution in our air, water and soil.

India Focus

21 Touch the Sky with Glory

The motto of the Indian Air Force is '*Nabha sprusham diptam*', which means to 'touch the sky with glory'. Its primary mission is to secure the Indian airspace.

Use the clues and the help box to find the names of aircraft in the Indian Air Force.

1. The Alouette III helicopter is called a faithful horse. ....

2. The Mirage 2000 is called a thunderbolt. ....

3. The Ilyushin II-76 is called the King of Elephants. ....

4. The Jaguar is called a type of sword. ....

5. The AN 32 is called the name of a river. ....

6. The MiG-29 is called the name of a predatory bird. ....

7. The Mi-17 is named after a brave Rajput King......................................

Help box

Gajraj	Vajra	Chetak	Pratap	Sutlej	Baaz	Shamsher

Whiz fact

The Gissar Military Aerodrome at Ayni in Tajikistan is India's first foreign military base. It was used by the Indian Air Force to evacuate Indians from Afghanistan during the Taliban takeover of the country in 2021.

22 Travelling to a Place Unknown

Most of us love travelling, but can you imagine travelling to an unknown place? People who do this are called explorers and they discover many new things on their voyages.

Fill in the blanks with words from the help box. Each exploration has two blanks.

1 .... was a Portuguese explorer who sailed west through the Pacific Ocean. He would have been the first to go around the globe but he was killed in a battle in the Philippines before his ship sailed back home across the ....

2 Marco Polo was an Italian merchant who travelled to ...., returned after 24 years, and wrote a detailed diary of his experiences called ....

3 Captain James Cook was a British naval officer who travelled to Newfoundland, Canada, and was the first European to reach ...., the eastern coast of Australia and the .... Islands.

4 Christopher Columbus travelled west from ...., completed four voyages across the .... and began the colonisation of the Americas.

Whiz fact

Leif Erikson was the first European explorer to reach continental North America. His father, Erik the Red, colonised Greenland in the 10th century.

5 On 29 May 1953, ... and .... were the first people to climb to the top of the highest peak in the world.

6 In 1909, American naval officer .... was the first to reach the geographic North Pole. Two years later, in December 1911, Norwegian explorer Roald Amundsen led the first expedition to reach the geographic ....

7 In the 1830s, a group of locals accompanied an Englishman named .... to a cluster of Hindu and Jain temples in the thickly forested Bundelkhand region of what is now Madhya Pradesh. The temples, named after the Sanskrit word for 'date palm', are the world famous site of ....

8 Two of the most sought-after destinations by intrepid but gold-hungry explorers have been .... in Colombia and .... in Tibet. They have never been found and are now considered mythical.

9 Vasco da Gama, the .... explorer, travelled east and reached .... by sea.

Help box

T S Burt/Khajuraho	Robert Peary/South Pole	Portuguese/India
Ferdinand Magellan/Indian Ocean	Asia/*The Million*	El Dorado/Shangri-La
New Zealand/Hawaiian	Europe/Atlantic Ocean	Tenzing Norgay/Edmund Hillary

STEM

23 Starry Skies

Read about astronomers and astronomical objects. Column A and Column C are already matched. Find the matching line about them in Column B.

Column A	Column B	Column C
1 Galileo, one of the first astronomers, explored space through a telescope.	a His model first placed the Sun at the centre of the solar system.	i They are now called Ganymede, Io, Europa and Callisto.
2 Ptolemy lived in Alexandria in the 2nd century CE.	b The planet is far more dazzling than actual stars and glows brightly.	ii Ptolemy's star charts were based on a model that put the Earth at the centre of the universe.
3 A pole star is used as a guiding star.	c He wrote an important text on 48 constellations.	iii In Indian astronomy, the pole star is called Dhruva.
4 Sirius is the brightest star in the night sky.	d He was the first person to discover four of Jupiter's moons.	iv In the *Harry Potter* series, the character Sirius Black could turn himself into a large dog.
5 Copernicus was a Polish astronomer and mathematician.	e It appears on the Australian flag in white.	v His heliocentric model influenced scientists like Galileo and Kepler.
6 Gerard Kuiper gave his name to the gigantic Kuiper belt.	f It is also called the Dog Star.	vi The Belt is one of the largest collections of objects in the solar system.
7 Venus is called the morning star as well as evening star.	g It is made of icy objects left over after the formation of our solar system.	vii But unlike a star, it does not twinkle.

World Around Us

24 Social Reformers

A social reformer is a person who tries to improve society or correct some wrongs in society.

Match the social reformers with the ills or rights they worked to abolish or fought for.

Social Reformer		Worked to abolish/fight for
1 Rosa Parks		a Sati in India
2 Raja Ram Mohan Roy		b Poorest of the poor in Kolkata
3 Maharani Gayatri Devi		c Untouchability in India
4 Nelson Mandela		d The rights of African Americans, especially women in the USA
5 Martin Luther King Jr		e African American rights in the USA
6 Mahatma Gandhi		f Women's education in Rajasthan
7 Mother Teresa		g Apartheid in South Africa

Life on Land

25 Plogging Away

Don't just slog away, plog away! Each piece of trash, especially plastic, that you pick up from the street, park, playground or any public place, could prevent a bird or an animal from choking, suffocating or getting caught on it.

Here are some facts about plogging. Join up the question and answer pairs to understand its story.

Questions

1. What is plogging?
2. Where does plogging come from?
3. What does "*plocka uppa + jogga*" mean?
4. Who invented plogging?
5. In which city did plogging first take place?
6. For what purpose did Erik Ahlström begin plogging?
7. How does plogging help as a workout?
8. How many people plog?
9. Who is Ripu Daman Bevli?
10. The banks of which urban river are being cleaned up using the efforts of local ploggers?

Answers

a. Erik Ahlström
b. More than 2 million people in 100 countries plog regularly.
c. It comes from the Swedish words '*plocka uppa*' and '*jogga*'.
d. The banks of the Mula-Mutha river are being cleared of plastic and medical waste by the Pune Ploggers.
e. It is an organised activity that combines collecting trash with body workout.
f. It means 'pick up + jog'.
g. He is a marathon runner who introduced plogging to India. He is also the ambassador of the FIT India Movement.
h. To rid the city of plastic waste, which is a global problem.
i. It is jogging combined with bending, squatting and stretching, and so the body movements are varied.
j. Plogging began in Stockholm, Sweden.

Whiz activity

Organise a plogging party with your friends in nearby park or a playground.

- Carry litter bags and hooks made from wire hangers to pick up trash.
- Remember to wear masks and gloves.
- Work in pairs while jogging.
- Pick up plastic wrappers or bottles and drop them into your litter bags.
- With the help of a trusted adult, throw the litter bags into a public garbage dump.
- Pat your backs for doing your bit for planet earth. ☺

26 Languages Across Countries

Here is a very interesting graphic that shows the number of speakers of the languages spoken most commonly in the world. Look at the infographic and say whether the statements are true (T), false (F) or not shown (NS).

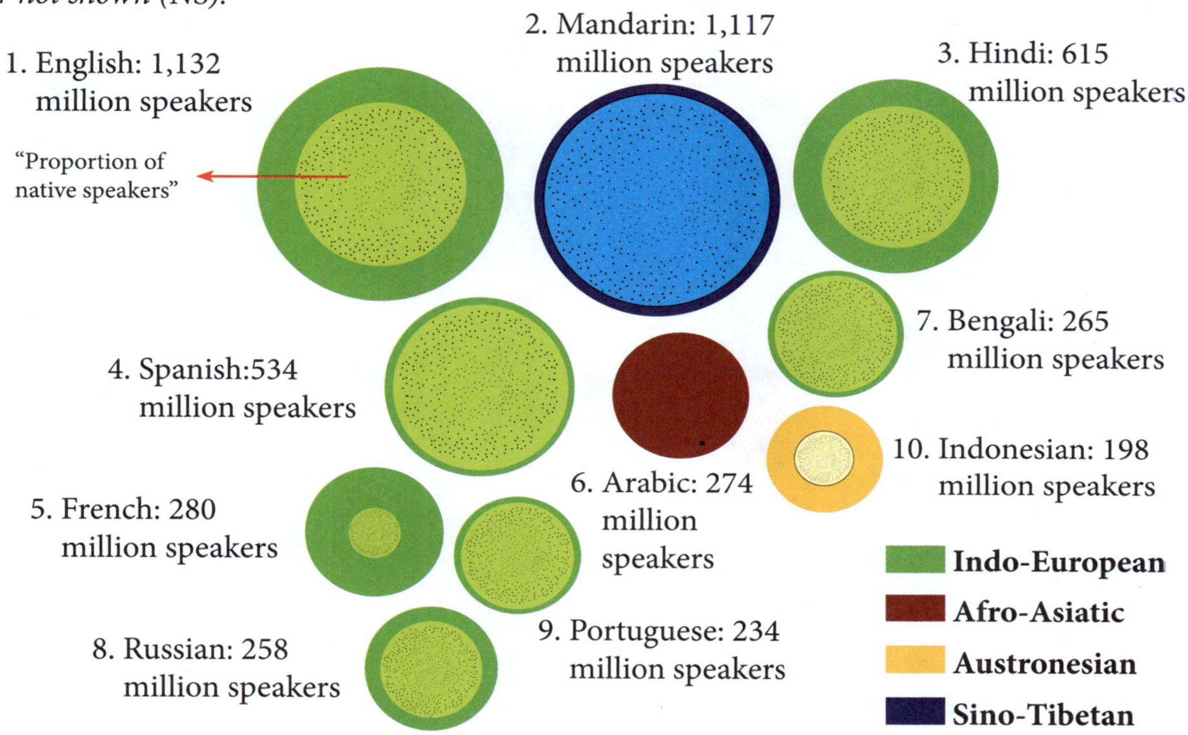

Statement	T/F/NS
1 There are more native speakers of English than Mandarin Chinese.	
2 Most of the top spoken languages in the world are of Indo-European origin.	
3 English is the most popular second language in the world.	
4 There are more French speakers in Africa than in Europe.	
5 Arabic is an Indo-European language.	
6 Four different linguistic groups are present in the list of top ten spoken languages.	
7 There are more Bengali speakers in India than elsewhere.	

Whiz quiz

Six of the top ten spoken languages around the world are UN languages. Name them.

1 .... 2 .... 3 .... 4 .... 5 .... 6 ....

27 Space Films

Space has always been a great inspiration for filmmakers.

Use the clues and the help box to identify the films and solve the crossword. Read down the highlighted column to find the name of yet another blockbuster space film.

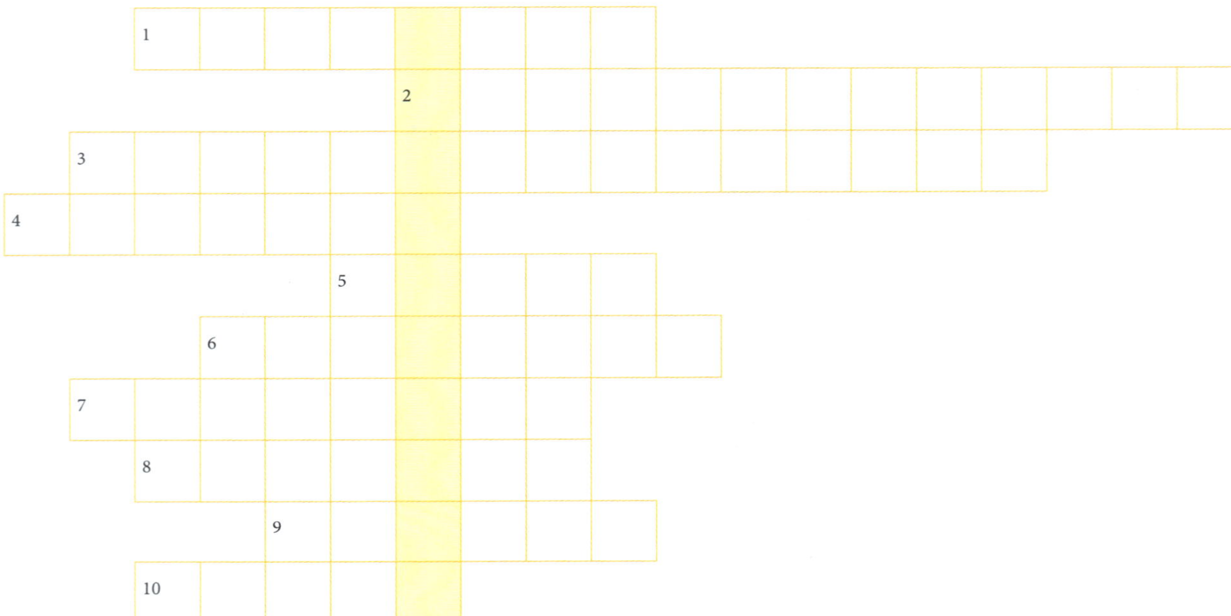

1 A biographical film based on the life of American astronaut Neil Armstrong.

2 The film tells the story of brilliant African-American women working at NASA who were behind the launch into orbit of astronaut John Glenn.

3 Diverse groups of people converge in the Nevada desert in the aftermath of a worldwide attack by an extraterrestrial race of unknown origin.

4 In this sci-fi film, Earth's citizens live in poverty, while the rich and powerful live on a gigantic, technologically advanced space habitat in the Earth's orbit.

5 An animated film about a solitary trash compactor robot who is left alone on deserted Earth to clean up garbage.

6 Captain Kirk and Vulcan Spock aboard the USS Enterprise combat the Romulan Nero, who threatens the United Federation of Planets.

7 An elite military rescue team is on a mission to save hostages who are being spied on, stalked and hunted by a technologically advanced space alien monster in Central America.

8 An engineer on her first space mission and an astronaut on his final expedition have to survive in space after they are hit by debris after spacewalking.

9 Humans are colonising a habitable moon of a gas giant in the Alpha Centauri star system and come across a humanoid species indigenous to the place.

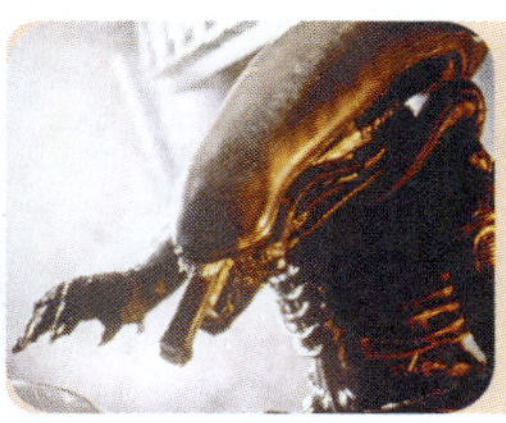

10 A horror film about a deadly and aggressive extraterrestrial set loose on a spaceship.

Help box

Alien | *Avatar* | *Elysium* | *First Man* | *Gravity*

Hidden Figures | *Independence Day* | *Predator* | *Star Trek* | *Wall-E*

Whiz fact

The Challenge is a 2023 Russian feature filmand includes sequences featuring professional actors filmed in space.

Natural World

28 Amazing Animal Traits

Animals have many amazing traits. For instance, hummingbirds are the only birds that can fly backward for any length of time. Of course, they can fly forward too.

Use the clues to solve the crossword.

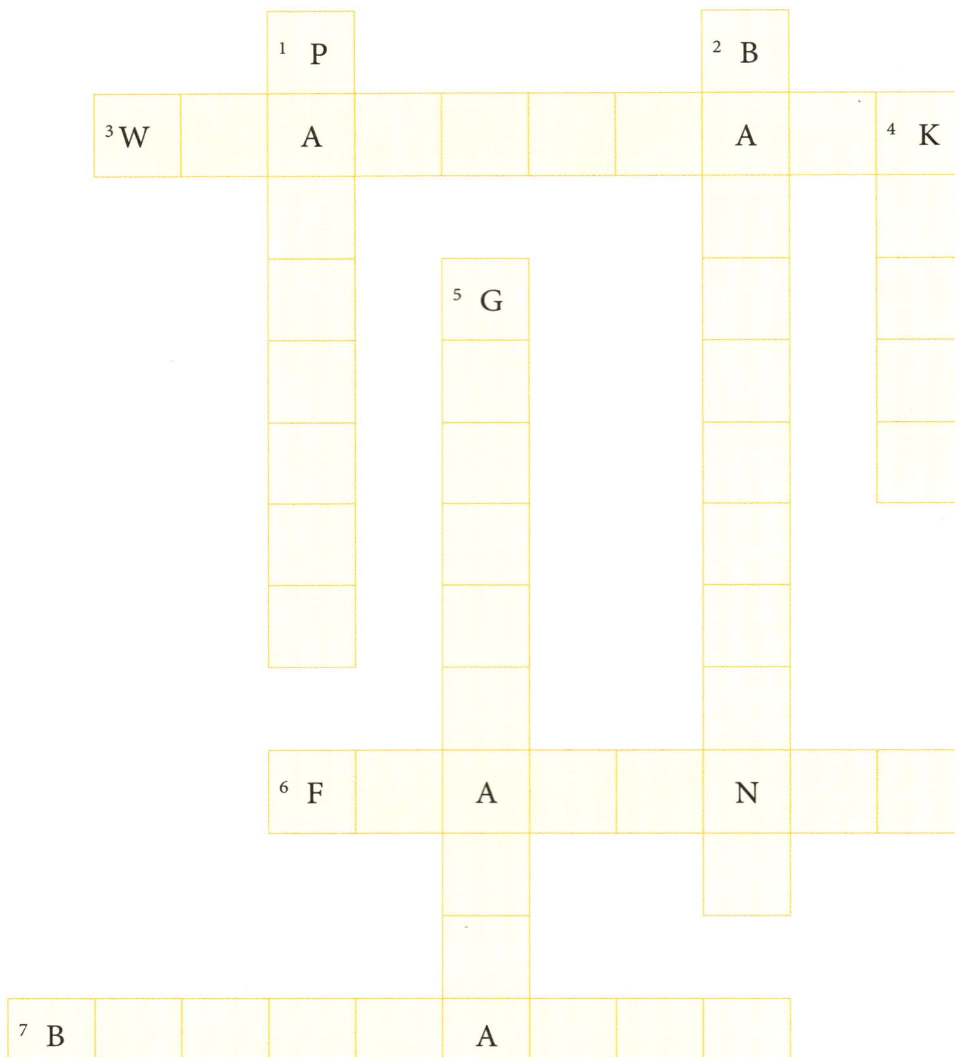

Across

3 This marine animal must move or it will drown. It survives because swimming is controlled by the spinal cord, so its brain can rest while the body continues to swim. (5, 5)

6 This bird is born white. It eats mostly salty shrimp, which makes it turn pink over time. (8)

7 This bird has feathers on its head. Its name comes from the Middle English word 'piebald', which means 'white feathers'. (4, 5)

Down

1 This animal has hard scales on its skin. It curls up into a tight ball to protect itself from predators. (8)

2 This dog breed is well known for hunting. Its droopy ears trap the scent of its prey for a long time. (6, 5)

4 Though it often has the word 'bear' attached to its name, this animal is related to the kangaroo family. It sleeps on tree branches for most of the day. (5)

5 This animal has flat, long molars so it can crush and eat bamboo shoots. (5, 5)

Whiz fact

The hummingbird is the only bird that can fly backwards. Some others, including egrets, herons and flycatchers, can flutter backwards for a very short while as a defensive action.

29 And The Award Is...

India Focus

Awards are one way to recognise the achievements of organisations and individuals.

Match the descriptions in Column 1 with the award names in Column 2 and the awardees in Column 3.

Column 1: Description

1. Given for outstanding literary work
2. The highest civilian award of the Republic of India
3. Given in the field of science
4. Given to individuals or organisations for promoting international peace and development
5. Lifetime achievement in sports and games, named after a famous sports personality

Column 2: Award

a. Shanti Swarup Bhatnagar Prize

b. Indira Gandhi Peace Prize

c. Sahitya Akademi Award

d. Dhyan Chand Award for Lifetime Achievement in Sports and Games

e. Bharat Ratna

Column 3: Awardee

i. Miss Bobby Aloysius, Athletics

ii. Aditi De, Quantum Information and Computing

iii. Centre for Science and Environment, independent research and advocacy think-tank

iv. Bhupen Hazarika, lyricist, poet, musician, film-maker

v. Devi Priya for *Gaali Rangu*, Telugu poetry

6 The highest sports award given to coaches for excellence in coaching	f Arjuna Award	vi Sakshi Malik, Wrestling
7 Given for outstanding contribution to the growth and development of Indian cinema	g Jnanpith Award	vii Cheteshwar Pujara, Cricket
8 Given for spectacular and most outstanding performance in the field of sports over a period of four years at international level.	h Dronacharya Award	viii Sumitranandan Pant, Hindi
9 Given to outstanding authors of creative literature	i Major Dhyan Chand Khel Ratna Award	ix Adoor Gopalakrishnan, Malayalam cinema
10 The most spectacular and outstanding performance by an individual sportsperson or team	j Dadasaheb Phalke Award	x Pullela Gopichand, Badminton

Whiz fact

Unlike the Nobel Prize, Indian awards can be given posthumously, that is, even after the death of the awardee. Subhas Chandra Bose was awarded the Bharat Ratna posthumously in 1992. However, as there was no evidence of his death, his family refused to accept the award as they believed that he was alive at the time. It is the only time in the history of the Bharat Ratna that the award was withdrawn.

30 Primates

Primates are different in many ways from other mammals, but the most important difference is that their brains are larger-than-average compared to their body size, and they are protected by larger-than-average skulls.

Use the clues to solve the crossword and find the names of different kinds of primates.

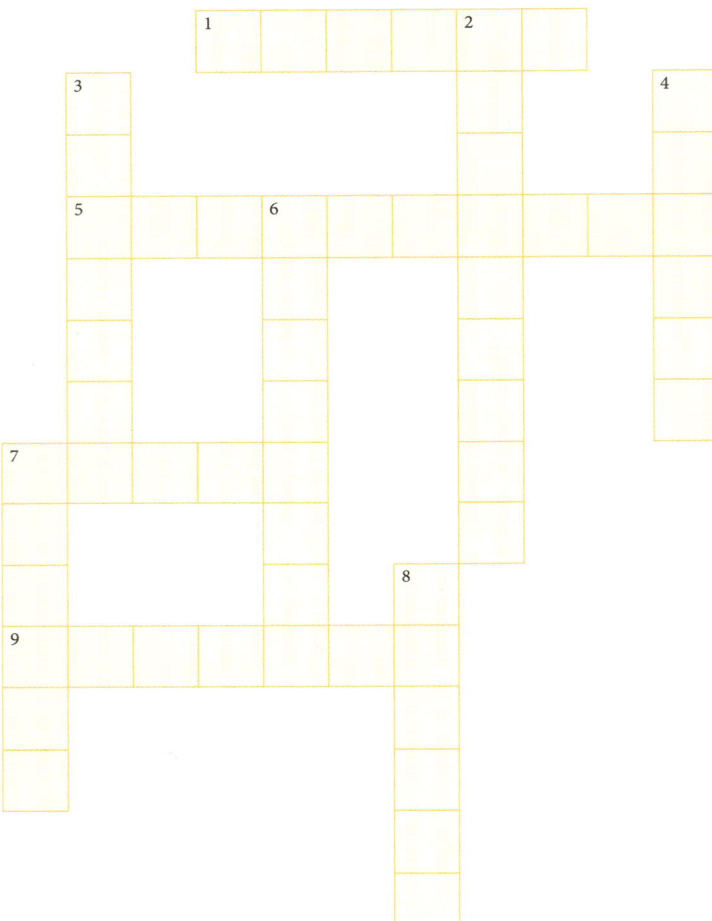

Gibbon

Orangutan

Chimpanzee

Gorilla

Lemur

Baboon

Macaque

Langur

Aye-aye

Mandrill

Across

1 This acrobatic primate swings gracefully, but is the most upright of the primates when it walks.

5 It is the closest living relative to humans, with 99% of their DNA in common.

7 Found in the wild only in Madagascar, one species of this is the only primate apart from humans to have blue eyes.

9 This largest living primate is primarily herbivorous and peace-loving, becoming aggressive only when threatened.

Down

2 The largest fruit-eating animal in the world, it rarely comes down from the trees.

3 All species of this primate are found in Asia, except one found in North Africa. Their arms and legs are of roughly the same length.

4 This nocturnal primate has claws like that of a sloth, incisors like those of a rodent, a body that looks like a monkey and a face that looks like a weasel.

6 It has a distinctive muzzle and is the largest monkey on Earth.

7 Its name means 'having a long tail'; it has white fur and a black face and it eats leaves.

8 A small yet social species of ape, it uses at least 10 different vocalisations to communicate.

Whiz quiz

Along with the common chimpanzee, this primate is the closest living relative of human beings. It is found south of the River Congo.

_ O _ O _ O.

Whiz fact

A nocturnal primate, the tiny tarsier has enormous eyes as large as its brain to enable it to see at night.

India Focus

31 Mayanagari Mumbai

Mumbai, formerly known as Bombay, is India's most densely populated city. It is the centre of business and entertainment. It has often been referred to as the 'city of dreams' for its vibrant pulse and entrepreneurial spirit.

Fill in the blanks using the words from the help box to know more about Mumbai. Use the same words to complete this acrostic.

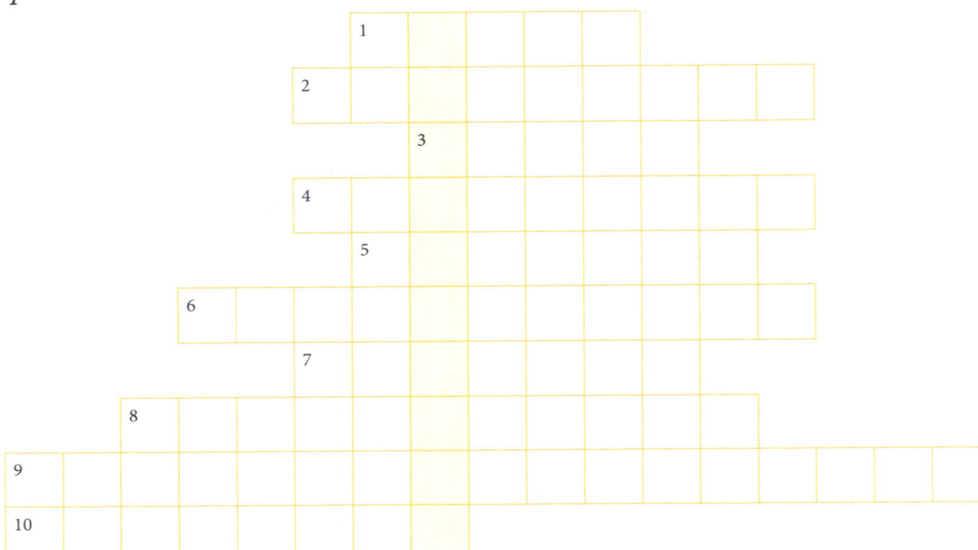

1 The first train in India ran from Mumbai to .... in 1853.

2 Also known as Gharapuri, the .... Caves are located on an island just off the southern coast of Mumbai.

3 The largest .... community in the world, which includes some of India's big industrialist families, lives in Mumbai.

4 Mumbai was 'given' away as the dowry of the Portuguese Princess .... of Braganza when she married Charles II of England.

5 The .... of India was built in honour of King George V when he visited Mumbai.

6 Also known as the Queen's Necklace, ... is a lovely coastal stretch of road with buildings on one side and the sea beyond a rocky shore on the other.

7 .... has the dubious distinction of being the largest slum in Asia, but gained fame as the setting for the Academy award-winning film, *Slumdog Millionaire*.

8 The Bombay Stock Exchange, the country's biggest stock exchange, is located on ....

9 The world's biggest film industry, the Hindi film industry, began its journey with the release of the mythological film .... by Dadasaheb Phalke.

10 Mumbai's spectacular Chhatrapati Shivaji Terminus, headquarters of the Central Railways, was originally called .... Terminus and is a UNESCO World Heritage Site.

Help box

Victoria | Elephanta | Catherine | Marine Drive | *Raja Harishchandra*
Parsi | Dalal Street | Dharavi | Gateway | Thane

Whiz quiz

Complete each of these lists with one word.

1 Chowpatty, Juhu, Gorai, Bhayender (B....... ....)

2 Worli, Bandra, Sewri, Dongri (F....... ....)

3 Apollo, Bori, Carnac, Arthur (B....... ....)

4 Sandhurst, Reay, Matunga, Currey (R....... ....)

5 Mahim, Thane, Vasai, Vashi (C....... ....)

Whiz fact

Mumbai was originally an archipelago of seven islands—Isle of Bombay, Colaba, Old Woman's Island, Mahim, Mazagaon, Parel and Worli. By 1845, these islands were joined by the process of land filling to form a single landmass. These islands are collectively referred to as *Heptanasia*, which is a Greek word for 'seven islands'.

32 British and American English

Language and Literature

The British brought the English language to the United States, but over time, the language developed differently in America. As a result, the same word is called by different names in British and American English.

For each item, fill in the missing word, whether it is British or American.

British word	Item	American word
1 Tap		....
2		Candy
3 Torch		....
4		Pants
5 Petrol		....
6		Pitcher
7 Pavement		....
8		Elevator

9 Queue

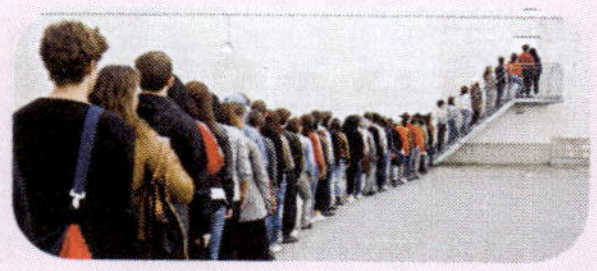

....

10 ....

Sweater

11 Chemist

....

12 ....

Vest

13 Crisps

....

14 ....

Cookie

15 Boot

....

16 ....

Truck

Help box

Trunk	Toffee	Flashlight	Biscuit	Waistcoat	Faucet	Sidewalk	Lift
Jug	Line	Potato chips	Gas	Druggist	Lorry	Trousers	Pullover

Whiz fact

British English uses 'our' in words like colour, labour and neighbour, while American English eliminates the 'u' to spell them with 'or' as color, labor and neighbor.

Life Skills

33 Measuring Tools

PROBLEM SOLVING

Measurements help us make sense of the world. Measuring yourself tells you which size of clothes you should wear; measuring your body temperature tells you whether you are sick or healthy; and measuring air temperature tells you whether you need to wear another layer before you go out.

Here are 12 measuring tools that we use every day. Use the clues, the images and the help box to find the names of each.

Clue	Item	Measuring Tool
1 Used to measure the temperature of the body and of food.	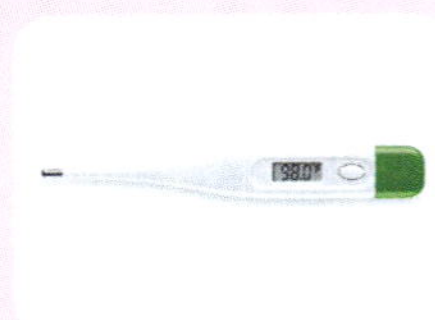	....
2 Tells us how heavy something is and is used for health checks and at airports.		....
3 Tells us how fast our vehicle is going so we can avoid fines by respecting traffic rules.		....
4 Lets us measure around body parts so we can find clothes that fit us.		....
5 Used to check whether we have enough air in our tyres, or whether our blood is flowing at the right pressure.		....
6 Tells us the total distance we have travelled, whether in a vehicle or in our fitness routine.		....

7 Helps to draw straight lines and also measures the length of things.

....

8 Helps measure how much of each ingredient to use in a recipe.

....

9 Tells us how much time we have to get ready, when to leave to catch the bus or whether we can finish a test in a given duration.

....

10 Tells us whether wall hangings are straight or not.

....

11 Tells us the direction in which we are heading.

....

12 Helps us cut a sheet of paper or see whether the wood is shaped right for a table top.

....

Help box

Measuring tape	Measuring cup	Square	Level	Clock	Speedometer
Pressure gauge	Compass	Odometer	Ruler	Thermometer	Weighing scale

Whiz fact

Gas meters and electricity meters measure how much gas and electricity have been used. These measurements are then used to generate the gas and electricity bills that we receive every month.

Sports

34 Extreme Sports

Extreme sports add an element of danger to the skills that any sport require. That's why it is so important to make sure you know the rules, have the right gear, prepare well and practise safety at all times when you're out having fun.

Match each sport with the correct image.

Clue

1 Slide down snow-capped mountains on a four-runner sled and you're bobsleighing.

2 Roll downhill inside a transparent ball made of elastic to absorb shock and you're zorbing.

3 Flying fox is sliding down through a zip line which is supported by a safety cable.

4 Paragliding is sailing above the earth to get a bird's eye view.

5 Caving lets you explore natural cave systems.

Sport

a 

b 

c 

d 

e 

6 Hot air ballooning involves getting a bird's eye view of the earth from the basket of a hot air balloon.

7 Clamber up or down natural rocks or artificial rock faces when you go rock climbing.

8 When you ride the waves on a board, you're surfing.

9 Mountain biking involves cycling on the rough terrain that mountains present.

10 Bungee jumping is when you literally drop off the edge of a cliff with just a rope tied around you to ensure you are not dashed to the ground.

f 

g 

h 

i 

j 

Whiz quiz

Name the extreme sport that

1 was developed in France by Raymond Belle.

2 is practised by a traceur or traceuse.

3 is a modified spelling of a term meaning 'course' (as in obstacle course), in which the 'c' is replaced by 'k' and the final 's' is dropped.

35 India's First Women

Here are some famous Indian women with firsts to their name.

Use the pictures, help box and descriptions as clues to identify them and fill in the blanks with their names.

1 The first Indian woman to get an aviation pilot licence and fly an aircraft. ....

2 She was the first Indian-born American woman to go to space. She lost her life in 2003 when the space shuttle *Columbia* was re-entering the Earth's atmosphere at the conclusion of a mission.
....

3 Called the Iron Lady of Manipur, she holds the record for the longest hunger strike (16 years), demanding that the Government repeal the act that gave the Indian Army special powers in Manipur. ....

4 Holder of an MBA degree, she left her corporate job to become the first woman sarpanch of India in Soda, a village 60 kms from Jaipur. ....

5 This banker is the first woman chairperson of the State Bank of India. ....

6 She was the first Indian woman to climb Mt Everest, in 1984. ....

7 She was the first woman to join the officer rank of the Indian Police Service in 1972. ....

8 The first Indian Miss Universe, she won the title in 1994.

....

9 India's first woman photojournalist, she was awarded the Padma Vibhushan in 2011. ....

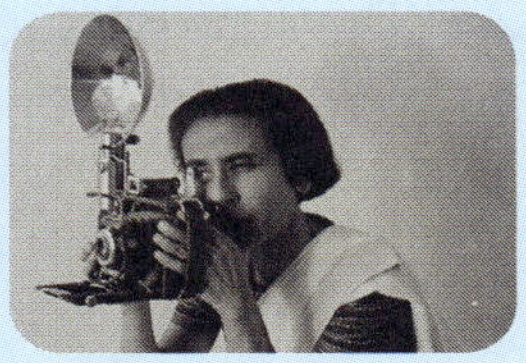

10 She was the first Asian woman and the youngest in the world to set a record in open swimming in Antarctic waters in 2015.

....

Help box

Kalpana Chawla	Irom Sharmila	Sushmita Sen	Kiran Bedi	Bhakti Sharma
Bachendri Pal	Chhavi Rajawat	Homai Vyarawalla	Sarla Thakral	Arundhati Bhattacharya

Whiz fact

A farmer's daughter from Assam, Hima Das, known as the Dhing Express, became the first Indian sprinter to win a gold medal at an international track event. She achieved this by winning the 400 m event at the World Under-20 Championship in 2018. A gifted footballer as well, she won five international gold medals in July 2019. She is UNICEF India's first ever youth ambassador.

Literacy Skills

36 Stamped!

Most stamps are printed on paper and affixed to envelopes or packages with glue.

Read about some unusual stamps and use the help box to fill in the blanks with the names of the countries.

INFORMATION

1 The cloth stamps from .... , the Gambia, Sierra Leone, and Saint Vincent and the Grenadines honour the humble teddy bear.

2 The stamp issued in .... features nocturnal animals and actually glows in the dark.

3 .... has a stamp in the shape of a banana.

4 This stamp from the .... contains a seed from the Ghaf tree.

5 The stamp from .... is coated with varnish containing microcapsules of coffee beans to commemorate the fact that the country provides most of the world's supply of coffee.

6 A souvenir set of stamps issued in .... was covered in beads on a sheet shaped like a handbag.

7 The stamp from .... gives off the scent of sandalwood.

8 .... issued the first ever stamp made of steel.

9 The stamp printed on thinly sliced cork is from ...., the European country that produces 30% of the world's supply of cork.

10 This stamp from the .... is actually a book which contains a complete story.

Help box

India, Bhutan, Netherlands, Grenada, Tongo, United Arab Emirates, Brazil, Malaysia, Portugal, Singapore

Whiz fact

Bhutan is known for its unusual stamps. In 1973, it issued self-adhesive Record Stamps which could be played on a gramophone. The stamps had Bhutanese folk songs and a short spoken history of the Kingdom. In 2008, Bhutan Post released the world's first CD-ROM postage stamps.

Affordable and Clean Energy

37 Energy Sources

Use the clues to find various sources of energy and solve the crossword.

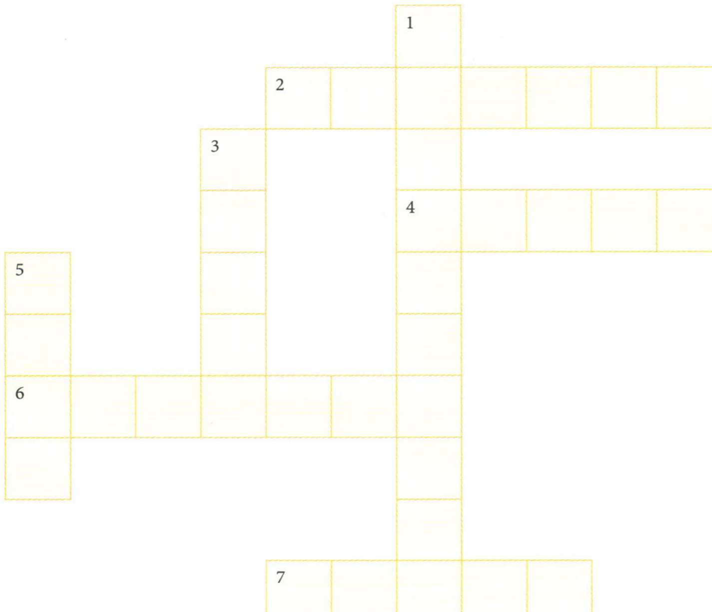

Across

2 This energy comes from the heat generated by the movement of tiny particles within an object.

4 This uses the power of ocean tides to generate electricity.

6 It comes from splitting atoms in a reactor to heat water into steam, turn a turbine and generate electricity.

7 This energy comes from people using panels on their homes to convert sunlight into electricity.

Down

1 This energy comes from the Earth's crust. Engineers extract steam or very hot water from the Earth's crust and use the steam to generate electricity.

3 When water flows through a dam or from a river, it activates a turbine, which runs an electric generator.

5 Turbines which look like giant windmills generate electricity from this energy source.

Whiz fact

Biomass is a source of energy. For his project of converting crop waste into biomass—and thus helping the environment in two ways—30-year-old Vidyut Mohan won the 2021 Earthshot Prize, considered the Green Nobel, awarded by his Royal Highness Prince William. It was accompanied by a cash prize of £1 million.

India Focus

38 Indian String Instruments

Fill in the blanks with vowels for the names of musical instruments and consonants for the names of musicians.

1. S .... N T .... R – This folk instrument from Kashmir is played by .... A .... U .... SHARMA.

2. S .... T .... R – This ancient instrument that flourished under the Mughals was popularised across the world by PANDIT .... I K .... I L BANERJEE.

3. .... K T A R .... – This one-stringed Bengali instrument is used by the folk singers of Bengal called BAU ....

4. S .... R B .... H .... R – This instrument has a lower tone than its more popular cousin, the sitar. K U .... A L DAS is one of its notable performers.

5. S .... R .... D – This instrument is descended from the Afghan rubab. A .... I AKBAR KHAN was one of its great exponents.

6. S .... R .... N G .... – Said to most resemble the sound of the human voice, USTAD .... U L .... A N KHAN was a notable performer of this instrument.

Whiz fact

The tanpura is a stringed instrument that does not play the melody but supports and sustains the melody of another instrument or singer.

Literacy Skills

39 Tech-wiz

TECHNOLOGY

Each of these sets contain three items that have something in common. Choose what they have in common from the options given.

1 PlayStation, Xbox and Nintendo Switch are all examples of what?

a Gaming consoles

b Home theatre systems

c Music players

2 CryptoLocker, Stuxnet and Leap-A are all variations of what?

a Cookies

b Viruses

c Trojans

3 Quince Tart, Red Velvet Cake and Snow Cone are versions of which OS?

a iOS

b Windows

c Android

4 ENVY, Spectre and Pavilion are all PCs manufactured by which company?

a Dell   b HP   c HCL

5 Vimeo, Twitch and Veoh are all types of what?

a Browsers   b Video streaming websites

c Video downloaders

6 Oasis, Paperwhite and Voyage are all versions of which product?

a Amazon Kindle   b Apple iPad   c Lenovo Yoga

7 Core, Coffee Lake and Apollo Lake are all processors made by which company?

a AMD   b Apple   c INTEL

8 Facebook, Instagram and WhatsApp are all apps owned by which company?

a Alphabet   b Meta   c Microsoft

9 Seasons, Rio and Space are all editions of which game?

a Temple Run   b Angry Birds   c Subway Surfer

10 Sega, Atari and Rockstar are all types of what?

a Video game companies   b Music apps

c Movie streaming apps

Whiz quiz

What was founded in Palo Alto in October 2003 by Andy Rubin, Rich Miner, Nick Sears and Chris White, and acquired by Google in July 2005?

Whiz fact

The social media platform Twitter was purchased by American billionaire Elon Musk in 2022 and renamed X. However, posts on X are still called tweets.

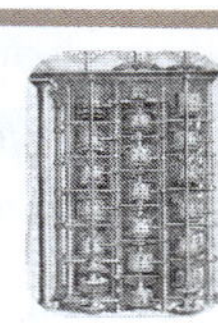

STEM

40 Science Shockers

The world is full of startling facts.

Match the facts in Column A with related ones in Column B.

Column A

1. A rabbit's teeth never stop growing.
2. If all the blood vessels of our body were laid out in a straight line, they would be about 1,00,000 kilometres long.
3. Capybaras, found in the Amazonian rainforests, are the largest living rodents in the world.
4. Many babies are born with blue eyes but later change colour.
5. Hippos are great swimmers. When they are completely underwater, their ears and nostrils fold shut to keep the water out.
6. Some people have synaesthesia, a condition that causes mixed signals from the sense organs.
7. The giant squid has huge eyes. Big eyes let in more light, allowing it to perceive even small contrasts in the depths of the ocean.
8. The fastest transmission of signals in the body happens in the alpha motor neuron in the spinal cord.

Column B

a. They can be as tall as German Shepherd dogs.

b. They wear down as it chews on grasses and vegetables, so that they never get too long.

c. Some of them can hear tastes, see smells, smell sounds, etc.

d. That is 2.5 times the circumference of Earth.

e. They can be as large as a human head.

f. Messages travel at speeds reaching upto 431 kilometres per hour.

g. They can hold their breath for up to five minutes underwater.

h. Eye colour is determined by a pigment which can take months to develop properly.

Whiz fact

Hair-Raising Facts:

- A human hair is stronger than a copper wire of the same diameter.
- After bone marrow, hair is the fastest growing tissue.
- When wet, hair can be up to 30% longer.
- A single hair lives for about 5 years.
- Most humans lose 50-150 strands of hair each day.

Natural World

41 Natural Disasters

Nature gives us all the essentials of life, such as air, food and water. But nature can also cause great destruction. When human meddling in nature oversteps its bounds, huge cataclysmic events, like the devastating bushfires of Australia and extreme heatwave conditions in the North American West Coast occur, causing enormous damage and discomfort.

Learn about some of the world's worst natural disasters by using the correct term from the help box to fill in the blanks.

1 The world's tallest tsunami occurred in 1958 in Lituya Bay, Alaska. It was .... tall, even taller than the Eiffel tower, which is 300 metres tall.

2 The Mt. Tambora eruption of 1815 is considered the worst .... eruption in the last one thousand years. It occurred in Sumbawa, an island of Indonesia, and released toxic gases that caused widespread climatic changes.

3 Chile experienced the worst earthquake ever in 1960. It measured .... on the Richter scale. Scientists estimate that this earthquake actually shifted the Earth's axis and made the day shorter by 1.26 microseconds.

4 Bangladesh was struck by the deadliest ever tornado in 1989. It destroyed more than 20 villages and killed around .... people.

5 The .... of China saw three very destructive floods in 1881, 1931 and 1938. They are collectively called the Huang He floods and they killed millions of people.

6 The eastern coast of Japan was struck by a massive earthquake in 2011. It destroyed large parts of Japan and killed about 16,000 people. Its effects were felt as far as Norway and ....

Help box

Antarctica | 1,300 | Yellow River | 9.5 | volcanic | 524 metres

Whiz fact

There were 399 natural disasters in 2023 around the world. India suffered 17 of these, mostly a combination of cyclones and floods. Overall, the number of natural disasters, exacerbated by human negligence or folly, has increased tenfold since the 1960s, with some 8000 adverse events in the new millennium alone.

42 Tribes of the World

A tribe is a group of people who have a common way of life. The modern world has encroached upon their land, forcing thousands of tribes to give up their way of life and integrate with the rest of the world. But there are still some tribes that retain their cultural identity.

Fill in the blanks with the correct answer. Use the picture clues and the words from the help box.

1. The Maori greet each other by rubbing their ....

2. The Kazakhs are excellent .... hunters.

3. The Huli of Papua New Guinea and Indonesia make and wear elaborate .... of their own hair and paint their faces.

4. The people of the Tarahumara tribe of Mexico can run for dozens of miles .... till they reach their destination.

5. The Asaro smear .... on their bodies to scare away warring tribes.

6. The Nenets of Siberia are known for .... herding.

7. The Maasai of Kenya and northern Tanzania are famous for their .... piercing and stretching.

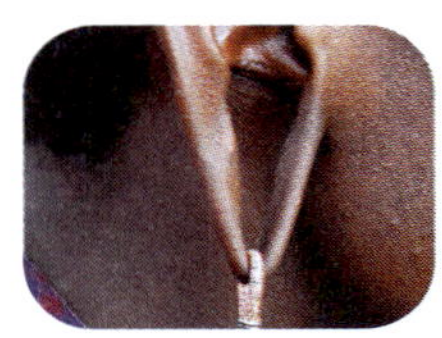

Help box

mud	ear	noses	barefoot	eagle	reindeer	wigs

Whiz fact

The people of the North Sentinel Island in the Andaman and Nicobar Islands have no contact with the outside world and live the way they have always lived since the dawn of humanity. They are among the most isolated people in the world.

STEM

43 Scientific Breakthroughs

Some scientific inventions have transformed the world.

Pick the correct option and fill in the blank with the correct answer.

1 Alexander Fleming accidentally discovered .... This ushered in the era of antibiotics, which cured previously deadly diseases. samoxycillin/penicillin

2 Louis Pasteur's germ theory uses heat to make wine, beer and milk safe for human consumption. This process is called .... pasteurisation/ sterilisation

3 German chemist Fritz Haber developed a process that was used to create a new class of fertilisers which greatly increased agricultural production. This increase is called the .... green revolution/white revolution.

4 Archimedes designed one of the first water pumps, which pushed water up a tube. This transformed .... and is used even today. water treatment/irrigation

5 The invention of .... later led to the creation of the microscope and the telescope. cameras/eyeglasses

6 In the early 20th century, scientists discovered botanist Gregor Mendel's 1866 paper. It helped them figure out how plant breeding works, and later, human .... worked. genetics/evolution

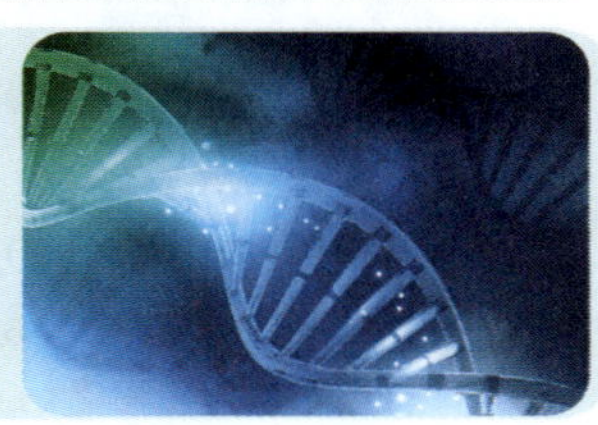

Whiz fact

Agriculture in the hard ground of Northern Europe and the American Midwest is only possible because of the mouldboard plough. This plough not only digs up the soil, but also turns it over, which allows crops to grow in it.

44 Constitution of India

India Focus

The Constitution of India is the supreme law of India. It lays down the instructions to be followed for the governance of the country. Here are some facts about the Constitution of India.

सत्यमेव जयते

1 The original Constitution of India was handwritten by Prem Behari Narain Raizada with beautiful calligraphy. Each page was decorated by artists from Santiniketan.

2 The Indian Constitution has 25 parts containing 448 articles and 12 schedules, and has 1,45,000 words, making it the longest written Constitution of any sovereign country in the world.

3 The Constituent Assembly took 2 years, 11 months and 18 days to come up with the final draft of the Constitution, and over 2,000 amendments were made to it before it was finalised.

4 The drafting of the Constitution was completed on 26 November 1949, but it was legally enforced two months later, on 26 January 1950, the day we now celebrate as the first Republic Day of India.

5 The handwritten Constitution was signed on 24 January 1950 by 284 members of the Constituent Assembly, which included 15 women.

6 The Preamble of our Constitution is an introduction to the purpose, aims and reasons for creating the Constitution.

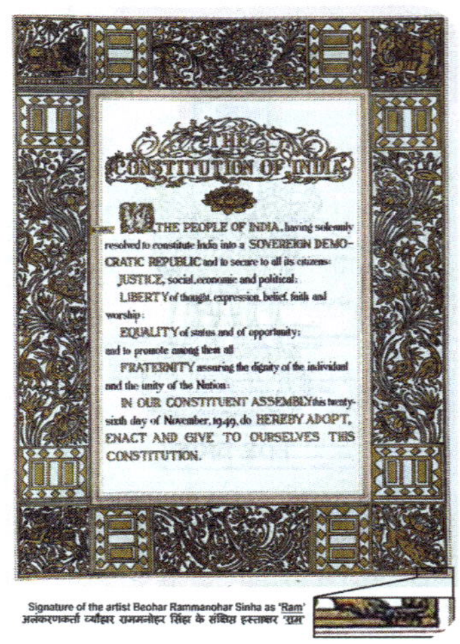

THE CONSTITUTION OF INDIA

WE, THE PEOPLE OF INDIA, having solemnly resolved to constitute India into a SOVEREIGN DEMOCRATIC REPUBLIC and to secure to all its citizens:

JUSTICE, social, economic and political;

LIBERTY of thought, expression, belief, faith and worship;

EQUALITY of status and of opportunity;

and to promote among them all

FRATERNITY assuring the dignity of the individual and the unity of the Nation;

IN OUR CONSTITUENT ASSEMBLY this twenty-sixth day of November, 1949, do HEREBY ADOPT, ENACT AND GIVE TO OURSELVES THIS CONSTITUTION.

Signature of the artist Beohar Rammanohar Sinha as 'Ram'
अलंकरणकर्ता व्यौहार राममनोहर सिंह के संक्षिप्त हस्ताक्षर 'राम'

7 The ideals of liberty, equality and fraternity in our Preamble have been taken from the French Revolution, which is also the French motto.

8 The Preamble to the Indian Constitution was inspired by the Preamble to the Constitution of the United States of America, which also starts with 'We the people'.

9 The fundamental rights recognised by our Constitution have also been adopted from the American Constitution. The Indian Constitution recognises nine fundamental rights as basic human rights of all its citizens.

10 The Indian Constitution was also influenced by the Constitutions of the United Kingdom, Ireland, Australia, Canada, the erstwhile Soviet Union, South Africa and Japan.

Read the facts and write whether the statements given below are true or false.

1 The Constitution of India was written by Dr B R Ambedkar. ....

2 The Indian Constitution was influenced by the Constitutions of Japan and Ireland. ....

3 The drafting of the Constitution of India was complete on 26 November 1949. ....

4 The Preamble to the Indian Constitution begins with the phrase 'We the people'. ....

5 The Indian Constitution recognises five fundamental rights as basic human rights of its citizens. ....

6 The Constitution of India was legally enforced on 26 January 1948. ....

Whiz quiz

How many members formed the Constituent Assembly that signed the handwritten constitution?

Whiz fact

Dr B R Ambedkar, the first law minister of free India, a jurist, economist and social reformer, was the Chairman of the Constituent Assembly that drafted the Constitution. He is often known as the 'Father of the Indian Constitution'.

World Around Us

45 Madagascar!

Madagascar is the fourth largest island in the world after Greenland, New Guinea and Borneo. It is situated in the Indian Ocean, about 400 miles away from the East Coast of Africa.

Use the clues and images to solve the crossword.

				1		2					
			3	E		I			4 A		
	5 Z		6	U							7 F
			A								
	8										
9	A		B						Y		
			B			10 A		E			E
11 M		L					Y				

Across

3 Madagascar is frequently called this because of the colour of its soil.

5 The local cattle of Madagascar

9 The long robe worn by men and women there

10 This rodent of Madagascar has an unusually large middle finger.

11 The national language of Madagascar

Down

1 Madagascar is home to this species of primate.

2 This animal is not found in Madagascar.

4 The currency of Madagascar

6 This tree has a bloated trunk which stores water.

7 Madagascar gained its independence from this country in 1960.

8 Madagascar is the world's largest producer of this flavouring agent derived from orchids.

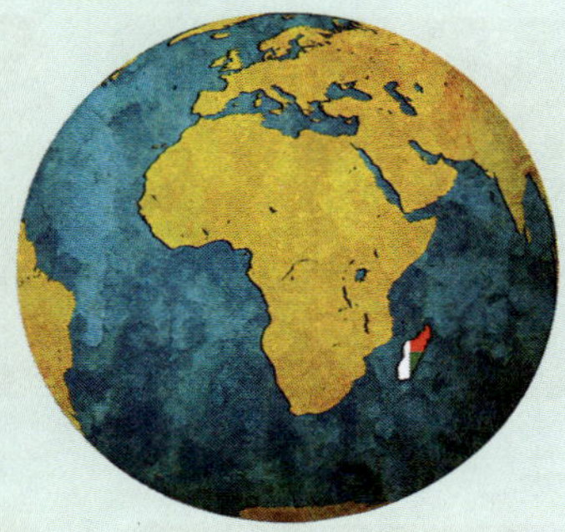

Whiz quiz

Match these names and guess the connection.

1	Ben Stiller	a	giraffe
2	Chris Rock	b	hippo
3	David Schwimmer	c	lion
4	Jada Pinkett Smith	d	zebra

Whiz fact

Native plants and animals in Madagascar evolved in relative isolation from the rest of the world. As a result, Madagascar is a biodiversity hotspot—over 90% of its wildlife is found nowhere else on Earth!

46 GI-tagged Products

The Geographical Indication (GI) tag is a certification which shows the distinctiveness of a product's origin at a particular geographical location and guarantees its quality. Items with the GI tag cannot be produced elsewhere.

Look at the pictures and read the descriptions about some GI tags from the northeastern part of India. Write the name of the product against each statement.

Muga silk

Wakro orange

Large cardamom

Chakhesang shawl

Bird's eye chilli

Khasi mandarin

Queen pineapple

Kachai lemons

Joha rice

Tree tomato

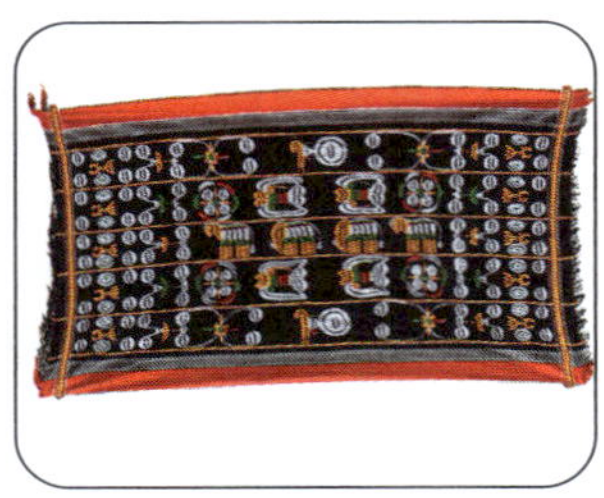
Saaphee lanphee

Moirang phee

1. Nagaland – One of the features of this Naga shawl is that the three pieces are woven separately and then stitched together. The central stripe is more decorated than the other two and the designs vary from a formal arrangement of lines, stripes, bands and squares to elaborate diamond and lozenge patterns. ....

2. Meghalaya – This citrus fruit with tight, smooth skin is very juicy and has a sweet, aromatic taste. ....

3 Tripura – This juicy fruit is not only GI-tagged and popularly tinned, it was also declared the state fruit of Tripura. ....

4 This spice is used in curries and rice preparations like pulao and biryani. ....

5 Arunachal Pradesh – The Lower Dibang Valley produces some of the best oranges in the country. ....

6 Mizoram – This chilli is small but quite hot. ....

7 Manipur – This citrus fruit of Manipur contains over 51% ascorbic acid, the highest of any citrus fruit grown in India. ....

8 Assam – This wild silk is known for its durability and extreme glossy texture. It was previously reserved for royalty. ....

9 Manipur – A textile with a sequential design woven with cotton or silk threads along the lengthwise edges and oriented towards the centre of the cloth. ....

10 Assam – A variety of rice known for its aroma, delicacy and excellent taste. ....

11 Manipur – Woven on indigenous looms, these shawls have animal and insect motifs hand-embroidered with cotton thread. ....

12 Nagaland – This egg-shaped edible fruit grows on trees. ....

Whiz quiz

Find out which state possesses a GI tag for these products.

1 Karbi Anglong Ginger ....

2 Memong Narang ....

3 Bhut Jolokia ....

4 Tezpur Litchi ....

Whiz fact

Northeast India has been identified as one of the world's richest biodiversity areas. Almost 70% of the world's orchids are found in this region.

Literacy Skills

47 How The Car Came To Be

Pick the correct word or phrase to know the story of how the automobile came to be.

INFORMATION

1 Almost 250 years ago, a French army engineer, Nicolas-Joseph Cugnot, built the world's first 'automobile', which used a steam engine to pull large horses/guns on the battlefield.

2 In 1807, French inventor François Isaac de Rivaz built a small automobile which had an engine that used hydrogen/petrol and CNG/oxygen as fuels.

3 In 1882, Italian inventor Enrico Bernardi fitted a petrol engine in his son's tank/tricycle, thus making it the first automated vehicle with a petrol engine.

4 The first 'modern' automobile was built in 1886 by German Karl Benz/Lagerfeld. This car used petrol as fuel.

5 In 1886, German inventors Gottlieb Daimler and Wilhelm Maybach also invented the first motorcycle/unicycle that year.

6 From then on, hundreds of companies started manufacturing cars across the world. In 1908, Toyota/Ford manufactured the Model-T, the world's first mass-produced car, which made it affordable for the public.

7 The first company to manufacture cars in India was Hindustan Motors, whose best known car was the Ambassador/Legacy.

8 Premier Auto started manufacturing cars as well and was well-known for manufacturing the Premier Lakshmibai/ Padmini, named after a legendary queen.

9 In the 1980s, the Maruti 800/1000, considered to be the first people's car, was launched by Maruti Suzuki.

10 Tesla/Ferrari makes electric cars which use sustainable energy.

Whiz fact

Rolls-Royce Limited was founded in 1904 by Charles Rolls and Henry Royce. Their cars have such good workmanship that over 65% of all Rolls-Royce cars ever built are still on the road! Rolls-Royce also makes jet engines for aeroplanes.

48 Scandinavia

Scandinavia is the name given to a cluster of five countries—Norway, Sweden, Finland, Denmark and Iceland.

Fill in the blanks with the correct names from the help box.

1 Norway is the world's largest exporter of ....

2 The .... appear above the Arctic Circle and are visible around the equinoxes in late September and March.

3 A Danish author who wrote many novels, plays and poems, ... is best known for his fairy tales.

4 Finland ranks high on several social and economic indices, and has secured the number one position in the World .... Report every year since 2018, an indication of the general well-being of the citizens.

5 .... from Denmark is the largest toy manufacturing company in the world.

6 There are no .... in Iceland.

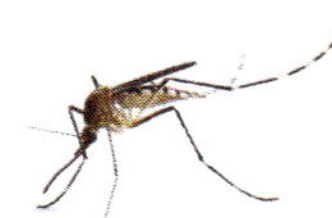

7 Norway's most famous author and playwright .... has not won the Nobel Prize for Literature, though three other Norwegian authors have been awarded the Nobel Prize.

8 .... is a Swedish brand that designs and sells ready-to-assemble furniture, kitchen appliances and home accessories.

9 The .... were the first inhabitants of Scandinavia. When the Finns, Swedes, Norwegians and Russians moved in, they moved further north into the area that is now usually known as Lapland.

10 Norway is often called the land of the .... because it has many of these long, narrow inlets of the sea, bordered by steep cliffs dug out by glacial erosion during successive Ice Ages.

11 The only mammal native to Iceland is the ....

12 ...., the Swedish chemist, engineer, businessman, philanthropist and inventor is the benefactor of one of the world's best known prizes for excellence in different disciplines.

13 The volcano .... erupted in the south of Iceland in March and April 2010 for the first time since 1821, causing many evictions and much disruption in air travel across Europe due to the ash clouds.

14 The Finns regard their country as the home of ...., who they believe lives in the northern region of Lapland.

15 .... is a 150-year-old amusement park in downtown Copenhagen. It is the most visited attraction in Denmark.

Help box

Alfred Nobel | Santa Claus | Tivoli Gardens | IKEA | Henrik Ibsen

Hans Christian Andersen | Arctic fox | salmon | Eyjafjallajökull

Northern Lights | Lego® | Happiness | mosquitoes | Sami | Fjords

Whiz fact

What do the English words 'crook', 'knife', 'husband', 'hell', 'plough', 'axle', 'window', 'raft' and 'leather' have in common? Among countless others, they are all from the Norse language spoken by the Vikings and thus of Scandinavian origin!

India Focus

49 Indian Nobel Laureates

The Nobel Prize acknowledges global contributions by an individual.

Find the missing portion of the names of eight Indian Nobel Prize winners from the help box and write them in the blanks given.

1 Subrahmanyan .... was an astrophysicist and nephew of C V Raman, who was awarded the Nobel Prize in Physics.

2 C V .... was a child genius who won the Nobel Prize in Physics.

3 Kailash ...., the founder of the Bachpan Bachao Andolan, won the Nobel Peace Prize in 2014.

4 Amartya .... received the Nobel Memorial Prize in Economic Sciences in 1998.

5 Har Gobind .... was awarded the Nobel Prize in Medicine.

6 Venkatraman .... won the Nobel Prize in Chemistry for his work on the ribosome.

7 Mother ...., founder of the Missionaries of Charity, won the Nobel Peace Prize in 1979.

8 Rabindranath .... was the first Asian to win a Nobel Prize in Literature.

Help box

Teresa   Raman   Ramakrishnan   Satyarthi
Chandrasekhar   Sen   Tagore   Khorana

Whiz fact

Mahatma Gandhi was nominated unsuccessfully for the Nobel Peace Prize five times. In 1948, when he was assassinated, nobody was awarded the Prize.

13 CLIMATE ACTION

Climate Action

50 Measures to Reduce Pollution

Many cities across the world are working innovatively to reduce pollution.

Use the clues to match the city to its pollution-reduction measures.

City	Measure to Reduce Pollution
1 Copenhagen is known as the bike capital of the world.	a Only a limited number of cars are allowed into the Swiss city at a time because there is no place to park them.
2 Curitiba in southern Brazil has a very low-cost bus system.	b Cars are not allowed on a large section of France's famous Right Bank of the river Seine.
3 Zurich has limited parking space in the city.	c For some decades, no vehicles are allowed on the roads of large parts of the Danish capital.
4 Paris bans cars in many of its historic areas (including around the river) on weekends and during special events.	d Roads have very little traffic and there is clear air because almost three-fourths of the people use buses to travel.
5 Bengaluru has reduced traffic pollution by changing the fuel used.	e The city aims to have almost no cars on the streets. They will ensure this by providing better public transport and allowing only walking and biking on inner city roads.

6 Freiburg, a city in Germany, makes car owners pay a huge sum of money to park on the edge of town. They are not allowed to park near their homes.

7 Helsinki aims to make its public transport so good that by 2025, the city will be almost car-free.

8 Oslo plans to reduce emissions by 95% by 2030 compared to 1990 levels, especially through charging motorists various types of fees.

f Emissions will be reduced by reducing the number of cars on the road. Levying heavy fees for driving during rush hour and congestion charges are some measures

g Because parking is so expensive, many are forced to live without a car. These people get free public transport.

h The city is moving away from petrol and using only Compressed Natural Gas (CNG) for its 6,000 buses.

Whiz quiz

Can you guess which Indian city has taken these measures to reduce pollution?

1 Banned use of diesel generator sets

2 Procured 1000 electric buses and 30,000 electric rickshaws

3 Procured 8000 bicycles, with the goal of eventually making 20,000 such cycles available

4 Installed continuous stack emission monitoring systems in industries

Whiz fact

The Paris Agreement, also called COP21, is an international treaty adopted in 2015 that aims to reduce the emission of gases that contribute to global warming.

India Focus

51 Victoria Memorial

British legacy in India lives on through the English language, the railways and postal system, but most visibly of all through the thousands of buildings built during the colonial period. One of the most lavish examples of British buildings is the Victoria Memorial in Kolkata.

Read this brief story and then write whether the statements are true or false.

A handsome pile of white marble in the heart of Kolkata, the Victoria Memorial is a monument built to honour Victoria, the Queen of England and Empress of India until her death in 1901. The memorial was commissioned immediately after her demise, but construction went on until 1921.

Victoria Memorial stands on Queen's Way close to a bank of the River Hooghly. If its dazzling whiteness reminds you of the Taj Mahal, it is because the marble used in its construction came from the same Makrana mines from which the material to build the Taj was quarried.

Lord Curzon, the then Viceroy of India, proposed the building of a museum and gardens, and appealed to the people to help in paying for the cost of construction. The people responded generously and the entire cost of ₹1 crore and ₹5 lakhs came from public funding.

When the Prince of Wales, later King George V, laid the foundation stone in 1906, Calcutta was the capital of India. But when it was finally built, it had been supplanted by Delhi, so the grand monument would forever grace but a provincial capital.

The Victoria Memorial sits amidst 64 acres of gardens scattered with statues of former Viceroys, allegorical sculptures representing justice, art, motherhood and a large bronze statue of the Empress herself sitting on her throne. An Angel of Victory sits atop the central dome of the memorial.

The galleries have some rare artworks and artefacts including the single largest collection of aquatints by renowned artists Thomas and William Daniell, the *Illustrated Works of Shakespeare*, the *Arabian Nights* and the *Rubaiyat* by Omar Khayyam.

In a crowded and noisy city, the Victoria Memorial stands in pristine white tranquillity, a green heart in the midst of bustling traffic, a monument to the rich but chequered history of Kolkata.

1. Victoria Memorial was built by the Empress of India.
2. Victoria Memorial was built using marble from Makrana.
3. The construction of Victoria Memorial was completed when Calcutta (now Kolkata) was the capital of India.
4. Lord Curzon laid the foundation stone for building the Victoria Memorial.
5. There is a statue perched on top of Victoria Memorial.
6. Thomas and William Daniell were well-known poets.
7. Works like the *Illustrated Works of William Shakespeare* can be found in the galleries of the memorial.

Whiz fact

The Taj Mahal and the Victoria Memorial were both built to honour Empresses, but after their deaths.

52 One and Only

Fill in each blank with one letter to find the answers to these interesting clues about countries around the world.

1 This is the only country in the world that doesn't have its own national anthem. In 1966, it decided to adopt neighbouring Greece's national anthem as its own. .... Y .... S

2 This is the only country in the world that has a musical instrument, a harp, as its emblem. I .... D

3 This is the only country in the world to be named after a woman.
S .... T L .... A

4 This is the only country in the world to have all five vowels occurring only once in its name. M .... E

5 This is the only country in the world where the pebble toad, which rolls itself into a ball and rolls like a pebble down the mountainous terrain, is found. V .... A

6 This is the smallest country in the world.
V .... N C .... Y

7 This is the only country in the world to be named after an element.
A .... A

8 This is the only country in the world to be named after a tree.
B L

9 This is the only country in the world to have a flag which has more than 4 sides. N L

10 The only country in the world where the gelada, a baboon-like monkey, is found. E .... A

11 This country has the maximum number of existing pyramids in the world. S .... N

12 This is the only country in the world whose name is also the name of a continent. A .... A

13 This is the only country in the world where voodoo is a recognised religion. H I

14 This is the only country in the world that has both lions and tigers in their natural habitat. I .... A

15 This is the largest country in the world with no rivers.
S .... I A .... A

16 This is the only country in the world that measures Gross Domestic Happiness (GDH) in addition to the Gross Domestic Product (GDP).
B .... N

Whiz fact

Only two countries in the world are double-landlocked. This means they are surrounded by one or more landlocked countries. They are Liechtenstein and Uzbekistan.

Sports

53 India at the Paris Olympics

The Summer Olympic Games take place every four years. Each edition of the Olympics takes its name from the host city.

Read these paragraphs about the Summer Olympics held in Paris.

Paris became only the second city, after London, to host the Olympic Games thrice- in 1900, then 1924 and now in 2024. The Games were conducted from 26 July to 11 August.

Manu Bhaker and Sarabjot Singh

117 Indian sportspersons competed in 69 events. India's medal tally was 6, one less than the 2021 Tokyo Olympics.

Shooter Manu Bhaker won two bronze medals, both in the 10m air pistol, one in the woman's event; and one in the mixed team event with Sarabjot Singh.

2021 Gold medallist Neeraj Chopra won the Silver in Javelin, losing to Pakistan's Arshad Nadeem.

Our other bronze medallists were wrestler Aman Sehrawat and shooter Swapnil Kusale.

44-year-old tennis player Rohan Bopanna was the oldest member of the Indian contingent.

14-year-old swimmer Dhinidhi Desinghu is the youngest Indian competitor.

Neeraj Chopra

Swapnil Kusale

Rohan Bopanna

Dhinidhi Desinghu

The Indian men's hockey team defeated Australia after 52 years in the Olympics, and won their second consecutive Olympic bronze. Their stars were goalkeeper Sreejesh and captain Harmanpreet Singh who scored 10 goals, the most at these Games.

Indian Hockey Team at Paris 2024

6 Indians finished fourth at the 2024 Paris Olympics:

Shooters Arjun Babuta, Manu Bhaker, archers Ankita Bhakat and Dhiraj Bommadevara, shooters Maheshwari Chauhan and Anant Jeet Singh Naruka, badminton player Lakshya Sen and Weightlifter Mirabai Chanu.

Arjun Babuta

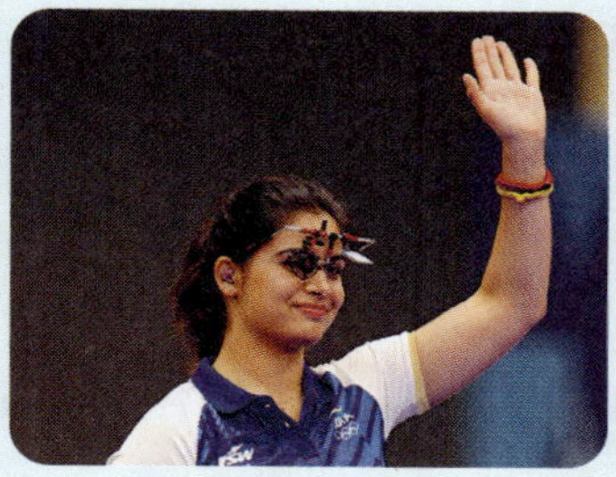

Manu Bhaker

Ankita Bhakat and Dhiraj Bommadevara

Maheshwari Chauhan and Anant Jeet Singh Naruka

Lakshya Sen

Mirabai Chanu

The next edition of the Olympics will be held in Los Angeles in 2028.

Statement		T/F
1.	Paris has hosted the Olympic Games more than any other city in the world.	
2.	The Indian Men's Hockey team won a medal at the Paris Games.	
3.	Indian wrestlers did not won medals at the Paris Olympics.	
4.	India won more medals in Paris than in Tokyo.	
5.	India won no gold medals at the Paris Olympic Games.	
6.	Neeraj Chopra won a silver medal in javelin throw at the Paris Olympics.	
7.	The Olympic Games are always hosted in cities that are national capitals.	
8.	Six Indian sportspersons won bronze medals at the Paris Olympic Games.	
9.	Manu Bhaker won more than one medal at the Paris Olympics.	
10.	India has won more Olympic golds in team sports rather than in individual sports.	

India Focus

54 India Tourism

India is a tourist's paradise, with innumerable places of interest to visit. Given below are some of the must-see places that have religious connection.

Match the image with its clue by writing the correct number in the boxes.

1 
Elephanta Caves

3 
Jain Temple at Talaja

5 
Sanchi Stupa

7 
Fatehpur Sikri

a One of the most revered places of worship for the Sikhs, it is located in Amritsar.

b This exquisite work of architecture resembling a budding nine-petalled lotus is the only house of worship of the Bahá'í community, located in New Delhi in India.

c Located a short distance from Mumbai, this UNESCO World Heritage Site is famous for its ancient rock-cut temples.

d This temple in Madurai is constructed in the typical Dravidian style.

e Located in Madhya Pradesh, it is a major pilgrimage site for Buddhists and was built by emperor Ashoka the Great.

f Located in the Bhavnagar district of Gujarat, they are known for their marvellous rock-sculpted exteriors.

g This historic town near Agra was built by Emperor Akbar and served as the capital of his empire from 1571 to 1585. The Tomb of Salim Chishti, a famous sufi saint, is situated inside the Friday Mosque Complex in this town.

h This Jewish house of worship in Kochi has exquisite chandeliers, coloured tiles, shiny brass pulpit and antique scrolls.

2 
Paradesi Synagogue

4 
Golden Temple

6 
Meenakshi Amman Temple

8 
Lotus Temple

Whiz fact

The 1000-year old Brihadeeswara Temple in Thanjavur, Tamil Nadu is part of the Great Living Chola Temples, a UNESCO World Heritage Site. The Government of India minted the first ever 1000 rupee coin to commemorate its millennial anniversary. In 2015, a second ₹1000 rupee commemorative coin was issued by the government in honour of the Nabakalebara Rath Yatra of the idols of the Jagannath Temple at Puri, Odisha.

55 Bridge Structures

Match the clues of bridge structures with their correct pictures by writing the correct letter in the boxes.

1 

Akashi-Kaikyo Bridge

2 

Astoria-Megler Bridge

3 

Godavari Bridge

4 

Ponte Vecchio

5 

Golden Gate Bridge

6 

Lowry Avenue Bridge

a. Beam bridges have one or several horizontal beams that span the area across the bridges.

b. Truss bridges use a diagonal mesh of mostly triangle-shaped posts above the bridge to distribute the force across almost the entire bridge structure.

c. Arch bridges use the arch as a main structural component, with the arch always being located below the bridge, never above it.

d. Tied arch bridges are similar in design to arch bridges, but they transfer the weight of the bridge and traffic load to the top chord that is connected to the bottom cords in bridge foundation.

e. Cantilever bridges are similar in appearance to arch bridges, but they suspend their load through diagonal bracing with horizontal beams that are supported only on one end.

f. Suspension bridges use spreading ropes or cables from vertical suspenders to hold the weight of the bridge deck and traffic.

Quiz Yourself 1

Answer these questions.

1 Which is the only country in the world that measures Gross Domestic Happiness (GDH) in addition to the Gross Domestic Product (GDP)?

(a) Bhutan (b) Switzerland
(c) Japan (d) Singapore

2 Which endangered animal can be spotted at the Hemis National Park in Ladakh?

(a) Lion (b) Snow Leopard
(c) Panther (d) Tiger

3 Which neighbouring country is well-known for its unusual stamps including the first self-adhesive Record Stamps and CD-ROM stamps?

(a) Pakistan (b) Bangladesh
(c) Nepal (d) Bhutan

4 For playing which Indian musical instrument is Hariprasad Chaurasia well-known?

(a) Bansuri (b) Santoor
(c) Sarod (d) Veena

5 Which island is the fourth largest island in the world?

(a) Borneo (b) Greenland
(c) New Guinea (d) Madagascar

6 Larisa Latynina won 18 Olympic medals for her performance in which sport?

(a) Swimming (b) Gymnastics
(c) Shooting (d) Athletics

7 In which country did Origami—an art form that involves paper folding—originate?

(a) China (b) South Korea
(c) Japan (d) Taiwan

8 Triskaidekaphobia is the fear of which particular number?

(a) 1 (b) 6
(c) 13 (d) 17

9 Which river flows through the city of Baghdad?

(a) Jordan (b) Amu Darya
(c) Tigris (d) Euphrates

10 For achievements in which field is the Shanti Swarup Bhatnagar Prize awarded?

(a) Sports (b) Science
(c) Cinema (d) Literature

Quiz Yourself 2

Answer these questions.

1. In which book do you find the characters the Tin Man, the Lion and the Scarecrow?
   (a) *The Wizard of Oz* (b) *Matilda*
   (c) *Oliver Twist* (d) *Charlie and the Chocolate Factory*

2. In which city in Brazil would you find the world-famous statue of Christ the Redeemer?
   (a) São Paulo (b) Brasilia
   (c) Rio de Janeiro (d) Manaus

3. Vehicles registered in which state would bear number registration plates beginning with 'ML'?
   (a) Mizoram (b) Madhya Pradesh
   (c) Manipur (d) Meghalaya

4. What were first place winners awarded along with a silver medal in the 1896 Olympics?
   (a) Gold crown (b) Olive wreath
   (c) Satin sash (d) Sword

5. Which is the only human infectious disease that has been completely removed or eradicated thus far?
   (a) Influenza (b) Smallpox (c) Chickenpox (d) Malaria

6. Which dance form is believed to be performed by a person bitten by the venomous spider, tarantula, under delirium?
   (a) Tarantella (b) Foxtrot (c) Tango (d) Waltz

7. In 1998, who became the first Indian to win the Nobel Price in Economics?
   (a) Raghuram Rajan (b) Amartya Sen
   (c) Abhijit Banerjee (d) Manmohan Singh

8. Which of these is the Japanese art of flower arrangement?
   (a) Bonsai (b) Manga (c) Ikebana (d) Shodo

9. What name is given to the inability to read correctly?
   (a) Myopia (b) Dysgraphia (c) Dyscalculia (d) Dyslexia

10. Which bone, the largest in the human body, can support 30 times the weight of a person's body?
    (a) Femur (b) Radius (c) Ulna (d) Tibia

Quiz Yourself 3

Answer these questions.

1. Who became the first Indian woman to climb Mt Everest in 1984?
   (a) Premlata Aggarwal (b) Santosh Yadav
   (c) Arunima Sinha (d) Bachendri Pal
2. The first case of which deadly disease was only recorded in 1981 but it has since spread across the world?
   (a) AIDS (b) Bird Flu
   (c) Rubella (d) COVID-19
3. Name the wooden toy who lived in Toyland with his friend, Big Ears, and drove a taxi for a living?
   (a) Peter Pan (b) Winnie (c) Noddy (d) Stuart Little
4. Apart from the Bonobo, which primate is the closest living relative to humans, with 99% of their DNA being common?
   (a) Gorilla (b) Chimpanzee
   (c) Orangutan (d) Macaque
5. Ice hockey is the national winter sport of Canada. What is its national summer sport?
   (a) Football (b) Rugby
   (c) Lacrosse (d) Basketball
6. Which of these musicians was awarded all four of India's civilian honours: the Padma Shri, the Padma Bhushan, the Padma Vibhushan and the Bharat Ratna?
   (a) Ustad Bismillah Khan (b) Pandit Shiv Kumar Sharma
   (c) Ustad Zakir Husain (d) Ustad Amjad Ali Khan
7. Which American swimmer has won 28 Olympic medals, including 23 golds?
   (a) Michael Phelps (b) Matt Biondi
   (c) Mark Spitz (d) Missy Franklin
8. Of which gas is dry ice, used in ice cream carts to keep ice cream cold, a solidified form?
   (a) Oxygen (b) Carbon Dioxide
   (c) Nitrogen (d) Carbon monoxide
9. The first 'modern' automobile was built in 1886 by which inventor?
   (a) Henry Ford (b) Karl Benz
   (c) Wilhelm Maybach (d) Charles Rolls
10. The world's largest lizard is the Komodo dragon. In which country is it found?
   (a) Malaysia (b) Indonesia (c) Myanmar (d) Thailand

Quiz Yourself 4

Answer these questions.

1 Which of these great leaders fought against an unjust system called apartheid in South Africa and was honoured with Nobel Peace Prize?
(a) Yasser Arafat (b) Fidel Castro
(c) Nelson Mandela (d) Aung San Suu Kyi

2 For playing which Indian musical instrument is Ustad Zakir Husain well-known?
(a) Bansuri (b) Santoor (c) Sarod (d) Tabla

3 Which fairy tale is immortalised by a bronze statue the waterside in Copenhagen, Denmark?
(a) *Snow White* (b) *The Little Mermaid*
(c) *Red Riding Hood* (d) *Tom Thumb*

4 Which Italian merchant from Venice travelled to Asia and stayed there for around 24 years?
(a) Christopher Columbus (b) Marco Polo
(c) Vasco da Gama (d) Amerigo Vespucci

5 In December 1911, which Norwegian explorer led the first successful expedition to reach the geographic South Pole?
(a) Roald Amundsen (b) Ernest Shackleton
(c) Robert Falcon Scott (d) Fridtjof Nansen

6 In Tokyo Olympics held in August 2021, how many events did India participate in?
(a) 50 (b) 45 (c) 34 (d) 69

7 Who was the first Indian woman to get an aviation pilot licence and fly an aircraft?
(a) Prem Mathur (b) Homai Vyarewala (c) Sarla Thakral (d)Durba Banerjee

8 Which European country has a musical instrument, the harp, as its emblem?
(a) Portugal (b) Ireland (c) Norway (d) Italy

9 What is the name of the adventure sport that involves rolling downhill inside a transparent ball made of elastic to absorb the shock?
(a) Zorbing (b) Zipping
(c) Bungee Jumping (d) Zip Rolling

10 Which kitchen appliance was invented by Percy Spencer in 1947?
(a) Mixer (b) Electric Oven
(c) Microwave Oven (d) Gas Stove

Answer Key

Page 9: 1. c; 2. g; 3. i; 4. h; 5. b; 6. j; 7. a; 8. e; 9. f; 10. d

Page 10: 1. Lisbon, Portugal; 2. Baghdad, Iraq; 3. Bangkok, Thailand; 4. Seoul, South Korea; 5. Madrid, Spain; 6. Warsaw, Poland; 7. Manila, Philippines; 8. Pyongyang, North Korea; 9. Belgrade, Serbia; 10. Damascus, Syria

Page 11: 1. Sumo wrestling; 2. Kabaddi; 3. Taekwondo; 4. Football; 5. Baseball; 6. Alpine skiing; 7. Golf; 8. Volleyball

Page 12: 1. road; 2. deer; 3. heir; 4. nose; 5. week; 6. write; 7. cereal, steel; 8. throne, would; 9. read; 10. Principal; 11. piece; 12. one, peak; 13. herd; 14. buy, blue, bread; 15. fare; 16. cents

Page 13: 1. Samba; 2. Dragon dance; 3. Zulu dance; 4. Polka; 5. Tango; 6. Ballet; 7. Flamenco; 8. Hip-hop

Page 14: I couldn't believe that I could actually understand what I was reading. Using the incredible power of the human mind, according to research at Cambridge University, it doesn't matter in what order the letters in a word are, the only important thing is that the first and the last letter be in right place. The rest can be a total mess and you can still read it without a problem. This is because the human mind does not read every letter by itself, but the word as a whole. Amazing, huh? Yeah and I always thought spelling was important!

See if your friends can read this too.

Page 15: 1. e; 2. g; 3. h; 4. f; 5. c; 6. d; 7. a; 8. b

Page 16-17: 1. b; 2. b; 3. b; 4. a; 5. a; 6. a; 7. b; 8. b

Page 18: 1. femur; 2. liver; 3. palms and soles; 4. make the eyes blink; 5. intestine; 6. Teeth; 7. feet

Page 19: 1. Gir; 2. Dachigam; 3. Eravikulam; 4. Keoladeo; 5. Hemis; 6. Chinnar; 7. Kaziranga; 8. Sundarban

Page 20: 1. irreversible, a baked caked cannot be turned into its ingredients again; 2. irreversible, crackers burnt cannot be used again; 3. reversible, salt can be obtained from water by the process of evaporation; 4. irreversible, sawdust cannot be turned into wood again; 5. irreversible, milk that turns sour cannot be good again; 6. reversible, shredded paper can be recycled as paper again; 7. can be reversible or irreversible depending whether the broken parts can be joined again; 8. irreversible, burnt coal turns to ash; 9. reversible, crushed bottles can be recycled again; 10. reversible, copper wires can be changed to sheets again; 11. reversible, melted broken glass can be joined again; 12. reversible, crumpled paper bags can be recycled

Page 21: 1. INFLUENZA; 2. CHOLERA; 3. MALARIA; 4. PLAGUE; 5. AIDS; 6. SMALLPOX; 7. TYPHUS; 8. YELLOW FEVER

Page 22-23: 1. b; 2. e; 3. a; 4. g; 5. c; 6. h; 7. d; 8. f; 9. p; 10. o; 11. m; 12. k; 13. j; 14. i; 15. l; 16. n

Page 24-25: 1. Cross country; 2. Rowing; 3. Gymnastics; 4. Swimming; 5. Fencing; 6. Sprinting; 7. Wrestling; 8. Kayaking; 9. Dressage; 10. Athletics; 11. Speed skating

Page 26-27: Across: 1. Dhole; 3. Orangutan; 5. Gharial; 7. Mexican Wolf

Down: 2. Komodo dragon; 4. Kakapo; 6. Blue whale; 8. Tarsier; 9. Bengal tiger; 10. Iberian lynx; 11. Pangolin

Page 28:

B	R	A	H	B	Z	E	I	G	E	R	N
K	E	T	T	L	E	S	C	H	W	Z	E
S	S	C	F	E	C	X	Z	P	O	I	V
A	T	L	R	N	A	I	A	U	I	A	O
L	R	U	V	D	Z	X	C	V	B	Q	E
F	X	M	B	E	T	R	T	R	Y	M	V
S	C	B	E	R	S	P	L	I	N	T	A
O	S	R	E	E	A	Q	C	X	U	I	W
M	E	Y	P	T	U	E	E	A	Q	X	O
R	O	T	A	R	E	G	I	R	F	E	R
E	R	L	S	T	R	V	A	W	A	C	C
H	G	A	S	S	T	O	V	E	E	A	I
T	M	N	K	L	Q	S	P	O	A	U	M

1. blender; 2. microwave oven; 3. thermos flask; 4. kettle; 5. refrigerator; 6. gas stove

Page 29: 1. Zakir Hussain, Krishan Maharaj; 2. Ravi Shankar, Nikhil Banerjee; 3. Ustad Amjad Ali Khan, Ali Akbar Khan; 4. Hariprasad Chaurasia, G S Sachdev

Page 30: 1. c; 2. d; 3. b; 4. a; 5. f; 6. e

Page 31: 1. Aqua; 2. Papyro; 3. Octo; 4. Auto; 5. Acro; 6. Arithmo; 7. Nocti; 8. Equino; 9. Somni; 10. Chromo; 11. Scoliono; 12. Megalo

Page 32: 1. T; 2. T; 3. T; 4. T; 5. F; 6. T; 7. T; 8. T; 9. F; 10. F; 11. T

Page 33: 1. Chetak; 2. Vajra; 3. Gajraj; 4. Shamsher; 5. Sutlej; 6. Baaz; 7. Pratap

Page 34-35: 1. Ferdinand Magellan, Indian Ocean; 2. Asia, *The Million*; 3. New Zealand, Hawaiian; 4. Europe, Atlantic Ocean; 5. Tenzing Norgay, Edmund Hillary; 6. Robert Peary, South Pole; 7. TS Burt, Khajuraho 8. El Dorado, Shangri-La; 9. Portuguese, India

Page 36: 1. d; 2. c; 3. e; 4. f; 5. a; 6. g; 7. b

Page 37: 1. d; 2. a; 3. f; 4. g; 5. e; 6. c; 7. b

Page 38: 1. e; 2. c; 3. f; 4. a; 5. j; 6. h; 7. i; 8.b; 9. g; 10. d

Page 39: 1. F; 2. T; 3. T; 4. NS; 5. F; 6. T; 7. NS

Page 40-41: 1. *First Man*; 2. *Hidden Figures*; 3. *Independence Day*; 4. *Elysium*; 5. *WALL-E*; 6. *Star Trek*; 7. *Predator*; 8. *Gravity*; 9. *Avatar*; 10. *Alien*

Page 42-43: Across: 3. Whale shark; 6. Flamingo; 7. Bald eagle

Down: 1. Pangolin; 2. Basset hound; 4. Koala; 5. Giant panda

Page 44-45: 1. c v; 2. e iv; 3. a ii; 4. b iii; 5. d i; 6. h x; 7. j ix; 8. i vi; 9. g viii; 10. f vii

Page 46-47: Across: 1.; Gibbon; 5. Chimpanzee; 7. Lemur; 9. Gorilla

Down: 2. Orangutan; 3. Macaque; 4. Aye-aye; 6. Mandrill; 7. Langur; 8. Baboon

Page 48-49: 1. Thane; 2. Elephanta; 3. Parsi; 4. Catharine; 5. Gateway; 6. Marine Drive; 7. Dharavi; 8. Dalal Street; 9. *Raja Harishchandra*; 10. Victoria

Page 50-51: 1. Faucet; 2. Toffee; 3. Flashlight; 4. Trousers; 5. Gas; 6. Jug; 7. Sidewalk; 8. Lift; 9. Line; 10. Pullover; 11. Druggist; 12. Waistcoat; 13. Potato chips; 14. Biscuit; 15. Trunk; 16. Lorry

Page 52-53: 1. Thermometer; 2. Weighing scale; 3. Speedometer; 4. Measuring tape; 5. Pressure gauge; 6. Odometer; 7. Ruler; 8. Measuring cup; 9. Clock; 10. Level; 11. Compass; 12. Square

Page 54-55: 1. e; 2. d; 3. a; 4. c; 5. b; 6. g; 7. h; 8. j; 9. f; 10. i

Page 56-57: 1. Sarla Thakral; 2. Kalpana Chawla; 3. Irom Chandu Sharmila; 4. Chhavi Rajawat; 5. Arundhati Bhattacharya; 6. Bachendri Pal; 7. Kiran Bedi; 8. Sushmita Sen; 9. Homai Vyarawalla; 10. Bhakti Sharma

Page 58-59: 1. Grenada; 2. Malaysia; 3. Tonga; 4. United Arab Emirates; 5. Brazil; 6. Singapore; 7. India; 8. Bhutan; 9. Portugal; 10. Netherlands

Page 60: Across: 2. Thermal; 4. Tidal; 6. Nuclear; 7. Solar

Down: 1. Geothermal; 3. Hydel; 5. Wind

Page 61: 1. Santoor, Rahul Sharma; 2. Sitar, Pandit Nikhil Banerjee; 3. Ektara, Baul; 4. Surbahar, Kushal Das; 5. Sarod, Ali Akbar Khan; 6. Sarangi, Ustad Sultan Khan

Page 62-63: 1. a; 2. c; 3. c; 4. b; 5. b; 6. a; 7. c; 8. b ; 9. b; 10. a

Page 64: 1. b; 2. d; 3. a; 4. h; 5. g; 6. c; 7. e; 8. f

Page 65: 1. 524 metres; 2. volcanic; 3. 9.5; 4. 1,300; 5. Yellow River; 6. Antarctica

Page 66: 1. noses; 2. eagle; 3. wigs; 4. barefoot; 5. mud; 6. reindeer; 7. ear

Page 67: 1. penicillin; 2. pasteurisation; 3. green revolution; 4. irrigation; 5. eyeglasses; 6. genetics

Page 68-69: 1. False; 2. True; 3. True 4. True; 5. False; 6. True

Page 70-71: Across: 3. Red island; 5. Zebu; 9. Lamba; 10. Aye-aye; 11. Malagasy
Down: 1. Lemur; 2. Hippopotamus; 4. Ariary; 6. Baobab; 7. France; 8. Vanilla

Page 72-73: 1. Chakhesang shawl; 2. Khasi mandarin; 3. Queen pineapple; 4. Large cardamom; 5. Wakro orange; 6. Bird's eye chilli; 7. Kachai lemons; 8. Muga silk; 9. Saaphee lanphee; 10. Joha rice; 11. Moirang phee; 12. Tree tomato

Page 74-75: 1. Guns; 2. hydrogen, oxygen; 3. tricycle; 4. Benz; 5. motorcycle; 6. Ford; 7. Ambassador; 8. Padmini; 9. 800; 10. Tesla

Page 76-77: 1. salmon; 2. Northern Lights; 3. Hans Christian Anderson; 4. Happiness; 5. Lego®; 6. mosquitoes; 7. Henrik Ibsen; 8. IKEA; 9. Sami; 10. Fjords; 11. Arctic fox; 12. Alfred Nobel; 13. Eyjafjallaökull; 14. Santa Claus; 15. Tivoli Gardens

Page 78-79: 1. Chandrasekhar; 2. Raman; 3. Satyarthi; 4. Sen; 5. Khorana; 6. Ramakrishnan; 7. Teresa; 8. Tagore

Page 80-81: 1. c; 2. d; 3. a; 4. b; 5. h; 6. g; 7. e; 8. f

Page 82-83: 1. F; 2. T; 3. F; 4. F; 5. T; 6. F; 7. T

Page 84-85: 1. Cyprus; 2. Ireland; 3. Saint Lucia; 4. Mozambique; 5. Venezuela; 6. Vatican City; 7. Argentina; 8. Brazil; 9. Nepal; 10; Ethiopia; 11. Sudan; 12. Australia; 13. Haiti; 14. India; 15. Saudi Arabia; 16. Bhutan

Page 86-87: 1. F 2. T 3. T 4. F 5. T 6. T 7. F 8. F 9. T 10. T

Page 88: 1. c; 2. h; 3. f; 4. a; 5. e; 6. d; 7. g; 8. b

Page 89: 1. f; 2. e; 3. b; 4. c; 5. a; 6. d

Page 90: Quiz Yourself 1: 1. a; 2. b; 3. d; 4. a; 5. d; 6. b; 7. c; 8. c; 9. c; 10. b

Page 91: Quiz Yourself 2: 1. a; 2. c; 3. d; 4. b; 5. b; 6. a; 7. b; 8. c; 9. d; 10. a

Page 92: Quiz Yourself 3: 1. d; 2. a; 3. c; 4. b; 5.c; 6. a; 7. a; 8. b; 9. b; 10. b

Page 93: Quiz Yourself 4: 1. c; 2. d; 3. b; 4. b; 5. a; 6. d; 7. c; 8. b; 9. a; 10.c